SUDDEN POSITION GUIDE TO
Acquisitions

ALCTS SUDDEN POSITION SERIES

Sudden Position Guide to Cataloging and Metadata, #1
Jeremy Myntti, Editor, 184 pp. 2019.
ALCTS, ISBN: 978-0-8389-4857-6

Sudden Position Guide to Cataloging and Metadata, #2
Becca Broday, Editor, 96 pp. 2020.
ALCTS, ISBN: 978-0-8389-4664-0

ALCTS SUDDEN POSITION SERIES #3

SUDDEN POSITION GUIDE TO
Acquisitions

Deborah Hathaway
Paul Kelsey
Stacey Marien
Susan E. Thomas

SUSAN E. THOMAS ■ SERIES EDITOR

Association for Library Collections & Technical Services
a division of the American Library Association
CHICAGO 2020

While extensive effort has gone into ensuring the reliability of information appearing in this book, the publisher makes no warranty, express or implied, on the accuracy or reliability of the information, and does not assume and hereby disclaims any liability to any person for any loss or damage caused by errors or omissions in this publication.

The paper used in this publication meets the minimum requirements of American National Standard for Information Sciences—Permanence of Paper for Printed Library Materials, ANSI Z39.48-1992.

ISBNs
978-0-8389-4849-1 (print)
978-0-8389-4850-7 (pdf)

Library of Congress Cataloging-in-Publication Data
Names: Hathaway, Deborah, author. | Kelsey, Paul, author. | Marien, Stacey, 1962- author. | Thomas, Susan E. (Librarian), author.
Title: Sudden position guide to acquisitions / by Deborah Hathaway, Paul Kelsey, Stacey Marien, and Susan E. Thomas ; Susan E. Thomas, series editor.
Description: Chicago : ALCTS Publishing, 2020. | Series: ALCTS sudden position series ; #3 | Includes bibliographical references and index. | Summary: "Depending on the structure of a library, acquisitions may involve or work with collection management, subject librarians, electronic resources, preservation, cataloging, and library administration due to the management and use of collection materials budgets. Acquisitions staff will also be involved in working with material library vendors. Taking on acquisitions responsibilities requires learning how to order materials in a variety of formats; learning basic accounting and budgeting practices; a knowledge of institutional fiscal and procurement policies and practices; along with strong communication skills as acquisitions librarians truly interact with staff in all library departments, as well as outside vendors. Some aspects of the work, such as managing collection budgets, allocations, expenditures, and encumbrances can at times be daunting, especially when end-of-year deadlines are looming. However, the variety of responsibilities that come with acquisitions make this one of the most rewarding service points in a library. If you have just taken on acquisitions responsibilities, you will want to understand the basic concepts and philosophy behind acquisitions work and develop an understanding for the day-to-day workflow"— Provided by publisher.
Identifiers: LCCN 2020044430 (print) | LCCN 2020044431 (ebook) | ISBN 9780838948491 (trade paperback) | ISBN 9780838948507 (adobe pdf)
Subjects: LCSH: Acquisitions (Libraries)
Classification: LCC Z689 .H38 2020 (print) | LCC Z689 (ebook) | DDC 025.2—dc23
LC record available at https://lccn.loc.gov/2020044430
LC ebook record available at https://lccn.loc.gov/2020044431

Copyright © 2020 by American Library Association. All rights reserved except those which may be granted by Sections 107 and 108 of the Copyright Revision Act of 1976.

Printed in the United States of America

24 23 22 21 20   5 4 3 2 1

The *Sudden Position Guide to Acquisitions* is dedicated to Dianne Rooney who was the longtime publications designer for the ALCTS Monographs Sudden Position Series and the ALCTS Sudden Selector's Guide series from ALCTS Publishing. The publication of this book would not have been possible without the hard work, dedication, and talent of Dianne.

Contents

FOREWORD *ix*
INTRODUCTION *xi*

One	**What You Absolutely Need to Know**	1
Two	**Standards and Best Practices for Acquisitions**	27
Three	**Things You Might Encounter**	51
Four	**Tools of the Trade**	63
Five	**Relevant Resources**	75
Six	**Conclusion**	83

ABOUT THE AUTHORS 85

Foreword

The *Sudden Position* series began with an idea from Mary Miller, Director of Collection Management and Preservation at the University of Minnesota, who was serving as the chair of the ALCTS Publications Committee. She suggested creating a monographic series similar to the ALCTS Collection Management Section (CMS)'s *Sudden Selector's Guide* series, but instead of focusing on resources, it would focus on the task of positions. As our profession evolves, many of us have experienced being asked to take on additional responsibilities. I found myself in this position over twelve years ago when one year into a new position managing collection development, I was asked to take on the responsibility for acquisitions. This was a new area for me, and I looked to ALCTS to help me get up to speed. I enrolled in the Fundamentals of Acquisitions web course, which I found extremely valuable in helping me to understand and take on this new responsibility. The *Sudden Position* series, like the Fundamentals web courses, is intended to provide the reader with essential knowledge, tools of the trade, and best practices in a concise, easy to read and reference narrative format. The guides are specifically meant to help anyone who is taking on a new position or added technical services responsibility.

Susan E. Thomas
ALCTS Monographs Editor
March 2020

INTRODUCTION
So You Are Suddenly Responsible for Acquisitions

Acquisitions manages the procurement of materials for the library's collection and is therefore a central function of any library. While obtaining items for the collection may seem as straightforward and easy as making a personal Amazon order, the steps involved for each item obtained for the library's collection will be varied and more complex. For example, if you are asked to order an item quickly, often referred to as a rush order, you will follow an established workflow that may involve verifying that the library does not already have the item, selecting the preferred format (electronic or paper), and determining which fund will be used to place the order against and through which vendor. You may use an electronic ordering system in your library that may require you to create a purchase order and download a MARC record. When the ordered item arrives, it may undergo a check-in process involving the paper invoice and the electronic ordering system. Some libraries review physical items for defects in order to return flawed items to the vendor for a refund or replacement before processing. After check-in, the item will then typically go to cataloging and labeling for use, unless it was ordered shelf-ready. While the item has gone through check-in and cataloging, acquisitions work will continue with the management and payment of the invoice. This workflow example for the acquisition of one item illustrates how complex the process can be to obtain materials for the library's collection. It is important to understand that for each step taken in the acquisitions process, there are underlying decisions, along with institutional policies and best practices to guide the process. While many of the basic concepts and tasks of acquisitions work will be applicable to any library, specific steps followed by each library may vary.

Depending on the structure of a library, acquisitions may involve or work with collection management, subject librarians, electronic resources, preservation, cataloging, and library administration due to the management and use of collection materials budgets. Acquisitions staff will also be involved in working with material library vendors.

Taking on acquisitions responsibilities requires learning how to order materials in a variety of formats; learning basic accounting and budgeting practices; a knowledge of institutional fiscal and procurement policies and practices; along with strong communication skills as acquisitions librarians truly interact with staff in all library departments, as well as outside vendors. Some aspects of the work, such as managing collection budgets, allocations, expenditures, and encumbrances can at times be daunting, especially when end-of-year deadlines are looming. However, the variety of responsibilities that come with acquisitions make this one of the most rewarding service points in a library. If you have just taken on acquisitions responsibilities, you will want to understand the basic concepts and philosophy behind acquisitions work and develop an understanding for the day-to-day workflow.

This *Sudden Position Guide to Acquisitions* will provide the "new to acquisitions" librarian with the information, tools, and resources needed to become familiar with the typical responsibilities of the position. Because acquisitions work can vary greatly among different libraries, the focus of this guide is not to be an exhaustive treatise, but rather to focus on providing a basic understanding of acquisitions work. Therefore, content of the guide focuses on the essentials, standards and best practices, things you might encounter, and tools of the trade. Acquisitions librarians will also want to become familiar with the *Core Competencies for Acquisition Professionals* developed by the Association for Library Collections & Technical Services Association (ALCTS) Acquisitions Section Education Committee in 2018. A number of resources listed in Chapter 5 will aid in providing additional knowledge and understanding of acquisitions.

Chapter **ONE**

What You Absolutely Need to Know

Acquisitions is the procurement and sourcing hub for libraries and typically involves ordering and receiving material in all types of formats, processing invoices, making payments, accounting, and managing material budgets. Work of the acquisitions librarian may also involve vendor negotiation, licensing electronic resources, working with MARC records, and facilitating access to materials leased or purchased. To make all of this happen seamlessly requires a sound knowledge of internal accounting and purchasing policies or rules, bookkeeping, allocation formulas, negotiating skills, searching skills, and use of electronic ordering systems.

WORKFLOW ORGANIZATION

Acquisitions will involve multiple workflows, and it helps to have the workflows written and organized in a manner that makes the documentation easily accessible. Many libraries are using LibGuides or Wikis to create an internal system to record workflows.

Ordering

Requests for purchases may come to acquisitions in a variety of ways. How libraries receive material requests to purchase may vary from one library to the next, and may be different based on the format requested. This list provides a sample of the ways an order may be given to acquisitions:

1. a vendor-specific ordering system, like Baker & Taylor or GOBI Library Solutions
2. web forms located on the library's web page
3. emails
4. circled items in a catalog
5. printouts given to acquisitions staff
6. verbally

The library should have procedures for placing the order with approved vendors. Procedures for ordering may vary from one library to the next and will most likely involve the use of an integrated library system (ILS).

Many publishing or library services vendors have their own ordering system that is used by both subject selectors and acquisitions staff. The ordering system should have help pages and tutorials, and many vendors are willing to set up training sessions either in person or through webinars. Even if the acquisitions librarian does not use the ordering system on a regular basis, it is recommended that the librarian become familiar with how it works. In many libraries, the acquisitions librarian is the point person to help the other selectors use the ordering system.

Firm Orders

Acquisitions librarians may place monograph firm orders through a library services vendor or directly with the publisher depending on the subject matter, availability, and discount offered. Firm orders are individual titles directly ordered by the acquisitions librarian from publishers or vendors using purchase orders and may be placed for eBooks or print titles. Vendors typically offer EDI (Electronic Data Interchange) or EOD (Embedded Order Data) software to place orders. Unlike a committed contractual expense or approval plan, they are one-time transactions. Returns for damaged or defective items are usually accepted, while returns for other reasons may incur additional shipping costs. Firm orders are typically placed for monograph titles, but one-time purchases for audiovisual materials, serial back runs, database content, or musical scores are also considered firm orders.

Firm order monographs are available directly from large publishers such as Oxford, Sage, Springer, or from vendors such as EBSCO or Amazon. Limited runs or out of print titles are sometimes difficult to locate from large suppliers, but may be available as a print-on-demand publication or from retail vendors such as Amazon or Alibris.

Before placing orders, the acquisitions librarian should factor in shipping costs, delivery time, whether it will need to be rebound, and accepted payment methods, as well as any applicable discounts. Discounts can be requested or negotiated with all publishers and vendors. The acquisitions librarian should plan on periodically reevaluating discount agreements and comparing pricing from all available vendors. In some cases, discounts for firm orders may depend on the quantity of items ordered. With firm orders, it is not possible to know in advance how many and what titles to order, and that gives the librarian less leverage in negotiating discounts. Additionally, some companies may have policies that do not allow the sales representative much negotiating room; however, there are two standard discount arrangements that every acquisitions librarian should know.

> **A flat discount** is based upon the volume of sales and type of materials ordered. It is applied for the entire account and not on a title-by-title basis. Its advantage is the predictability of allowing the librarian to know the discount up front. Flat discounts have the potential to be higher than those applied title by title, because the discount is based on purchase volume. Another

disadvantage is that some companies may require a certain number of purchased volumes or that they become the library's primary vendor. Some vendors may have publishers that are exempt from the discount, such as academic publishers, and discounts are not often applied for rush materials.

A sliding scale discount is applied title by title based upon a formula granted by the publisher to the vendor. Its main advantages are that it provides a more accurate representation of the true costs of the title, and as it is not based on volume sales, every library receives the same discount. The disadvantage is its unpredictability; some titles may receive a discount while others remain priced at retail value.

Acquisitions librarians should also keep in mind that they may occasionally see platform hosting fees for electronic formats, MARC record fees, and an added service fee to firm print monograph orders. While more common in academic libraries than public libraries, an added service fee is a surcharge placed by the vendor on the purchase price if there are increased shipping charges, or if there is increased effort needed to fill the order (i.e., contacting the author of self-published books, rush requests).

Serials and Databases

Acquisitions departments are set up differently depending on the size of the library. In some small libraries, the acquisitions librarian may be responsible for ordering serials (print and electronic) and databases. However, at many larger academic libraries, the acquisitions librarian is in charge of print serials and eBooks, and it is the electronic resources librarian who is responsible for electronic journals and databases. Some libraries may also have a separate serials librarian. If the new acquisitions librarian has little to no experience with serials, it is important to become familiar with the workflow and understand how acquisitions interact with other departments in the library. Who is responsible for what role in each department? How are new titles ordered and by whom? What ILS system is used and how are the titles checked into the system? Who is responsible for receiving requested serials? Is claiming for journal issues done, and if so, by whom? Where are the titles shelved? Are the back issues bound, and if so, who pulls the volumes to send out for binding? What happens with issues not bound? Are the journal titles kept in closed or open stacks? The answers to these questions will assist in creating a skilled and productive acquisitions department.

A library's mission is to build a dynamic collection that meets the current and future needs of its users, while the primary goal in acquisitions is to acquire and provide the continued access to relevant and ongoing resources. Both of these objectives must be carried out within the fiduciary framework of the materials budget. Databases are desirable by libraries as they complement the print and electronic serial holdings. Aggregated databases, whether subject specific or multidisciplinary, provide collections of electronic journals and eBooks, usually with full-text availability from publishers and associations. As the full-text content depends on deals struck with the publishers by the database producers, the addition of new titles and the deletion of others may result in users and librarians not always aware of the database content. Embargoing, which provides access to older journal content, but not the most current issues or volumes, is another problem with aggregated databases.

Databases are contractual obligations and are either subscribed to or purchased. If purchased outright, there may still be annual hosting fees to account for in the budget. Many libraries authorize the acquisitions librarian to negotiate pricing directly with the vendor and sign contracts and licenses, while others may have to work with the procurement or business office. For renewals, most database vendors require a signed order renewal form authorizing an invoice sent at the beginning of the renewal period. Many database vendors offer a discounted or locked rate for a multi-year contract. Additionally, some vendors provide an auto-renewal option for invoicing without reviewing the order. While this may sound like a time-saving measure, it may not be easy to adequately budget or renegotiate terms with the auto-renewal process. It is essential for the acquisitions librarian to thoroughly understand department roles and responsibilities when working with contractual obligations and the requirements before signing and authorizing purchases or renewals. Additionally, the acquisitions librarian should look over the contract for the following clauses and flag areas of concern for the negotiation process.

- **Indemnification:** *Licensor agrees to indemnify* is the best option as it legally and financially protects the library. Ask to remove the clause or language that requires the licensee to indemnify the licensor, otherwise condition the clause with "to the extent permitted by the laws of the State of ____."
- **Governing law:** applicable to U.S. law is the best choice, especially when dealing with foreign-based parent companies
- **Limitation of claims:** no limitation of claims is the best option
- **Terms:** clearly stated renewal period, price, and payment terms
- **Authorized users:** clearly outlined who can or cannot access
- **Interlibrary Loan:** ILL rights permitted and method of electronic provision not restricted is the best option
- **Course packs/reserves:** electronic reserves allowed, record-keeping and deletion requirements clearly stated
- **Perpetual access:** (if applicable) hosting fees specified
- **Usage statistics:** COUNTER compliant is the best option
- **Concurrent users:** number of concurrent users specified
- **Archival rights:** free or price specified
- **MARC record availability:** supplying entity named; cost specified if not free

Factors affecting the acquisition of serials include format, either print or electronic, content availability, and budget. They are acquired, either as bundled packages or institutional subscriptions directly from large publishers, serials vendors, such as EBSCO, and individually for smaller press journals. More and more content is offered online in various packages, and the savvy acquisitions librarian will weigh current collection practices against the pros and cons of bundled deals before making a decision to cancel print subscriptions for electronic bundled packages.

A bundled deal is typically an arrangement between a library and a publisher, vendor, or consortia to purchase electronic access to all its journals for a discounted per-journal basis versus a pick-and-choose ala carte institutional pricing model. Its primary advantage is that library users gain access to many more journals than previously offered. However, this benefit may also be a disadvantage if the titles are not relevant to users. For this reason, it is important to acquire the title list before committing to a bundled deal; compare the titles included against duplication with current print subscriptions as well as other bundled packages.

Serials management is typically unique to the individual library due to the nature of its workflow. Journals, journal packages, newspapers, microfilm, and periodicals are all ordered and received into the ILS, but not all libraries check-in print publications. While labor intensive, for large serial collections, checking-in print serials enables librarians to monitor changes in publication frequency and patterns, claim missing issues, track those ready for binding, as well as provide a history of any publication name changes.

Many libraries use a serials vendor subscription service such as EBSCO, Harrassowitz, or WT Cox to manage serial subscriptions. In cases where the serial is not available through a vendor, the library will need to subscribe directly with the publisher. A vendor management provider offers the benefit of centralized management for all serial resources and usually includes link resolution, an A-Z search list, collection analysis tools for usage and download statistics, and MARC records. When evaluating the services offered by a subscription service provider, the acquisitions librarian should ask about coverage, serial change notifications, activation and licensing, if invoices are delivered electronically, what usage data is provided, and how to make cancellations.

ERMs (electronic resource management) open source systems, such as CORAL (Central Online Resources Acquisitions and Licensing), are another option for managing all electronic resources. CORAL is available free of charge and includes several modules that are both customizable and run independently of each other. Libraries can pick and choose which modules best meet their library's needs.

FUND IDS/CODES AND TRACKING FUNDS

Ledger Structure

One-time purchases (firm orders) versus continuations (serials) can also have separate funds for approvals, reserves, media, standing orders, collection maintenance, binding, bibliographic records, shipping costs, taxes, and miscellaneous categories such as consortia purchases. Each category can be separated by fund code and then format. Here are a few examples showing how funds might look in different systems.

Example of ledger from Voyager:

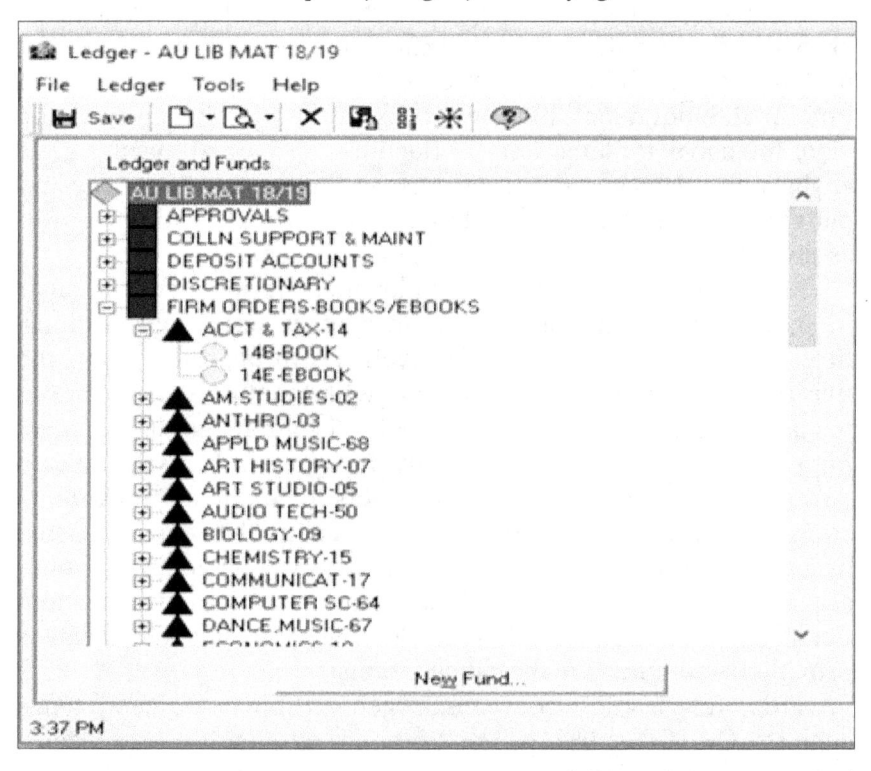

```
Ledger - AU LIB MAT 18/19
File  Ledger  Tools  Help
  Save

Ledger and Funds
  AU LIB MAT 18/19
    APPROVALS
    COLLN SUPPORT & MAINT
    DEPOSIT ACCOUNTS
    DISCRETIONARY
    FIRM ORDERS-BOOKS/EBOOKS
        ACCT & TAX-14
            14B-BOOK
            14E-EBOOK
        AM.STUDIES-02
        ANTHRO-03
        APPLD MUSIC-68
        ART HISTORY-07
        ART STUDIO-05
        AUDIO TECH-50
        BIOLOGY-09
        CHEMISTRY-15
        COMMUNICAT-17
        COMPUTER SC-64
        DANCE.MUSIC-67

                                    New Fund...
3:37 PM
```

WHAT YOU ABSOLUTELY NEED TO KNOW **9**

Another ledger example from SirsiDynix might look like this:

Fund ID	Fund Name	Cash Balance	Cash (%)	Free Balance	Free (%)	Budgeted	Encumbered	Invoiced	Paid
Total		$801186.32	88%	$553017.22	61%	$905866.66	$248169.10	$0.00	$104680.34
BINDING	BINDING - BK...	$1605.90		$1600.90		$2000.00	$0.00	$0.00	$394.10
DBASES	Databases	$365977.59	81	$365977.59	81	$450000.00	$0.00	$0.00	$84022.41
DBASES_PREP...	Pre-paid Librar...	$0.00	0	$0.00	0	$2785.67	$0.00	$0.00	$2785.67
DEPT_FUNDS	Funds provided...	$0.00		$0.00		$0.00	$0.00	$0.00	$0.00
DONATIONS	Donations	$0.00		$0.00		$0.00	$0.00	$0.00	$0.00
ELEC_BOOK	Electronic Books	$54648.54	94	$54648.54	94	$57889.00	$0.00	$0.00	$3240.46
ENG_STROUD	M-ES - Monogr...	$4750.63	100	$4750.63	100	$4750.63	$0.00	$0.00	$0.00
FREEDOM PROJ...	Dr. Sullivan's a...	$7695.90	100	$7695.90	100	$7695.90	$0.00	$0.00	$0.00
GIFTS	Gifts	$0.00		$0.00		$0.00	$0.00	$0.00	$0.00
MISC_INC	MISCELLANEO...	$0.00		$0.00		$0.00	$0.00	$0.00	$0.00
MLIB	Library Associa...	$7992.02	100	$7992.02	100	$7992.02	$0.00	$0.00	$0.00
MONO_ART	M-ART - Art	$2344.18	94	$2344.18	94	$2500.00	$0.00	$0.00	$155.82
MONO_BIO	M-BIO - Biology	$1000.00	100	$1000.00	100	$1000.00	$0.00	$0.00	$0.00
MONO_CLASS	M-CLA - Classics	$1300.00	100	$1300.00	100	$1300.00	$0.00	$0.00	$0.00
MONO_DRAMA	M-DRA - Drama	$300.00	100	$300.00	100	$300.00	$0.00	$0.00	$0.00
MONO_EDU	M-EDU - Educat...	$500.00	100	$500.00	100	$500.00	$0.00	$0.00	$0.00
MONO_FREN	M-FRE - French	$128.35	43	$128.35	43	$300.00	$0.00	$0.00	$171.65
MONO_GERM	M-GER - German	$2500.00	100	$2500.00	100	$2500.00	$0.00	$0.00	$0.00
MONO_HIST	M-HIS - History	$3959.14	99	$3920.37	98	$4000.00	$38.77	$0.00	$40.86
MONO_HIST LA...	History of Latin...	$0.00		$0.00		$0.00	$0.00	$0.00	$0.00
MONO_HIST S...	History & Scien...	$500.00	100	$500.00	100	$500.00	$0.00	$0.00	$0.00
MONO_HUMAN...	Department Hu...	$800.00	100	$800.00	100	$800.00	$0.00	$0.00	$0.00
MONO_ITAL	M-ITA - Italian	$2000.00	100	$1969.51	98	$2000.00	$30.49	$0.00	$0.00
MONO_LIB	Library - gener...	$6055.76	98	$5992.28	97	$6200.00	$63.48	$0.00	$144.24
MONO_MLMF	Library Monogr...	$1404.35	100	$1404.35	100	$1404.35	$0.00	$0.00	$0.00
MONO_MUSIC	M-MUS - Music	$1000.00	100	$1000.00	100	$1000.00	$0.00	$0.00	$0.00
MONO_PHIL	M-PHI - Philoso...	$3111.42	89	$3111.42	89	$3500.00	$0.00	$0.00	$388.58
MONO_POL	M-POL - Politics	$3459.72	99	$3459.72	99	$3500.00	$0.00	$0.00	$40.28
MONO_REPL	M-REP - Replac...	$1951.63	99	$1951.63	99	$1973.46	$0.00	$0.00	$21.83
MONO_SOM	M-SOM - Schoo...	$800.00	100	$800.00	100	$800.00	$0.00	$0.00	$0.00
MONO_SPAN	M-SPA - Spanish	$1500.00	100	$1500.00	100	$1500.00	$0.00	$0.00	$0.00
MONO_THEO	M-THE - Theology	$1500.00	100	$1500.00	100	$1500.00	$0.00	$0.00	$0.00
MONO-COMP	Computer Scie...	$300.00	100	$300.00	100	$300.00	$0.00	$0.00	$0.00

Common Ledger Vocabulary

Commitments: value of all outstanding purchase order encumbrances

Encumbrance: an amount of money set aside to pay for items on order but not yet received

Pending commitment: value of all unapproved purchase orders

Expenditures: value of all approved invoices/vouchers (amount spent to date)

Pending expenditures: value of all pending invoices/vouchers

Balances available: budget—total commitments/expenditures

Balances cash: net allocation—total expenditures (What is actually available if encumbrances are not factored.)

Expenditures total: value of all approved invoices/vouchers (i.e. spent to date)

Expenditures pending: value of all pending invoices/vouchers

Balances available: net allocation—total expenditures

Balances cash: net allocation—total expenditures

Acquisitions Accounting

- An invoice without a commitment will decrease Available & Cash balances upon approval.
- An invoice against a commitment will decrease Cash balance but will not affect the available balance.
- For a system that does not use encumbrances (such as serials) in order to see funds available, one must manually subtract pending invoices from Available or Cash.
- A pending purchase order assigns dollars to pending commitment, i.e., $100 spent on a pending PO=$100 pending commitment.
- An approved purchase order moves dollars to total commitment, i.e., $100 on an approved PO=$100 total commitment.
- A pending invoice assigns dollars to total commitment and pending expenditures, i.e., $100 pending invoice = $100 total commitment AND $100 pending expenditure.
- An approved invoice assigns the dollars to total expenditure, i.e., $100 approved invoice = $100 total expenditure and $0 total commitments and $0 pending expenditure.

Modifying and Transferring Funds

At the beginning of a new fiscal year, allocations (the amount of money determined for a particular fund code) are entered as new funds in the ledger. How allocations for each fund are determined may vary from one library to the next. Some libraries use complex formulas or may incorporate the previous year's spending. The acquisitions librarian will need to monitor fund balances throughout the year. A negative balance in any fund should be avoided. Most systems will allow for transfers between funds to cover deficits, for purchase orders to be overridden if fund balances are negative, or for the addition of new money into a fund. Sources of new money may come from many sources including non-library department transfers if sharing the cost of a subscription or firm order purchase. Ultimately, the goal is to have funds fully expended at the end of the year but exact accounting practices may vary from one institution to the next.

Each ILS may have a slightly different ledger in terms of features and structure. The first thing a new acquisitions librarian should do is to become familiar with the ledger, the meaning of terms used, and how it works. It is important to understand how the money moves through the ledger, from initial commitment with establishment of an order to payment. Encumbrances, pending invoices, paid invoices, and free balance all monitor available funds. The ledger will show two areas—one for encumbrances or commitments and one area for expenditures.

Invoices

The acquisitions librarian should be familiar with the ways an invoice is received from the vendor. Invoices may arrive electronically from the vendor, with the shipment, or may be sent through the post. It is important to have checks and balances when dealing with the invoices, just as it is with ordering and receiving. Typically, the person who creates the invoice is not the person who signs or approves the invoice. Optimally, three people should be involved. One person receives the invoice, a second verifies the invoice, and a third person signs the invoice. In many libraries, the acquisitions librarian has the authority to sign the invoice (and in smaller libraries, may possibly create and receive the invoice). Once the invoices are signed, they are ready for payment. Libraries may vary on the procedures followed for payment of invoices. It is important to note that invoices are often time sensitive and should be paid within thirty days of receipt. In many libraries, there are two financial systems working parallel to each other. There is the ILS that the library uses and then there may be a financial system used by the larger organization, which may be more typical for academic libraries.

Budgeting is an integral component of a library's vision for growth, services, and other administrative decisions. One of the most challenging responsibilities facing the acquisitions librarian is creating and allocating the materials budget. A carefully planned budget ensures that funds are available and assigned to all resources offered by the library. Libraries face increasing pressure to justify budgets and demonstrate a return on investment (ROI). While the library director has the ultimate authority and responsibility for the total library budget, the acquisitions librarian plays a pivotal role in budget discussions, as they are responsible for overseeing the materials budget and expensing it strategically. Strategic budgeting involves not only understanding the total amount available and what percentages to allocate but also an understanding of the effect, to both the budget and services provided, if asked to reduce or eliminate portions of the budget. A successful acquisitions librarian must be proactive and engage in conversations with vendors regarding new products, license agreement renewals, and negotiate discounts, as well as continually evaluate current resources to determine usage and return on investment.

The annual budget for library acquisitions, commonly referred to as the materials or collections budget, encompasses all funding or revenue allocated by the governing organization and any additional funds from outside sources. Revenue and expenses are the two sides that must balance in any materials budget. There are many methods available for creating material budgets with the three most common covered in this section. However, the acquisitions librarian should remember that a properly and strategically planned budget helps decide the success or failure of an organization's strategic plan. The budget acts not only as a control measure to keep from spending too much but also as a vital planning element for determining how an organization will allocate its resources both in the present as well as for the future. A successful acquisitions librarian will look at all budgeting methods, inquire which the organization is using, and choose the method or combination of methods that best serve the library.

Audits

Accounting within an organization indicates a need to be aware of auditing requirements. Depending on the institution and level of authority, acquisitions will most likely have some role in maintaining records in the event of an audit. The specific auditing requirements will vary by institution and may involve working with an accounts payable department. Maintaining records of all transactions is important, especially when asked to provide additional documentation to answer questions about an invoice. The librarian may be asked to retrieve the invoice as well as any supporting documentation, such as a packing slip for the item. As an acquisitions librarian you will want to learn what information should be kept for audits along with the retention requirements. Many institutions are moving toward electronic maintenance of invoices where invoices sent electronically are saved to a designated online folder, or if received as paper, are scanned and uploaded to a file. Electronic files can facilitate easy access and the sharing of information when needed. In other cases, invoices are kept in paper format and may have to be held for several years.

Budget Systems Explained

Incremental line-item budgeting is one of the most common and widely used budget systems as it is simple to create and maintain. However, its simplicity is also a disadvantage when attempting to make changes to the budget, therefore, think carefully about using it for strategic budgeting. Incremental line-item budgeting assigns increases and decreases equally across the entire budget based on a percentage regardless of how they fit into the strategic plan.

Formula budgeting is a method of apportioning the materials budget to various departments based on predetermined factors of importance to the organization. Formula budgeting is a historical method of allocating funds in many academic libraries, and there are numerous studies available on this process, including the ACRL formula guidelines for academic institutions. Formulas are useful for determining allocations; however, the acquisitions librarian needs to remember this is only a tool. Knowledge of the strategic plan, as well as, the strengths and weaknesses of the collection and the role each department has in regard to the strategic plan is central to deciding how to allocate the budget. Typical elements used in most academic formulas include:

- Departmental need
- Current collection level in each subject
- Cost of materials
- Terminal degree offered (i.e., bachelor, master, Ph. D.)
- Major or concentration only
- Number of declared students, number of faculty
- Teaching method (i.e., lectures involving library research, laboratory using online databases and little library use, etc.)

Zero-based budgeting (ZBB) is a system in which all expenses must be justified at the beginning of each fiscal year without consideration of any previous spending; it is the opposite of an incremental line-item budget. Essentially, the acquisitions librarian creates each fiscal year budget with a zero base instead of a set figure and justifies every line item before allocating funds. A zero-based budget system allows the budget to accurately reflect what is needed based on a careful analysis of the performance of the prior fiscal year, and it identifies expenses no longer necessary. Many institutions are implementing zero-based budgeting as a way to control the overall budget by requiring justification for all line items from every department. Zero-based budgeting is somewhat problematic for libraries who typically have contractual commitments for serials and standing orders and have little control or foreknowledge of renewal pricing. However, while this method does require a significant investment of time, it allows the acquisitions librarian to think strategically and shift funding to where it is most useful now and in the future.

Developing the Budget

In developing a materials budget, the first step is to identify the total amount available for materials and then determine the total financial funding necessary to continue offering resources. It is helpful to compare the prior year's budget with the proposed budget. Once final budget numbers for the fiscal year are set, the acquisitions librarian will begin to construct a budget with anticipated expenditures for the year. Expenditures may be divided by line items, programs, or funds. Note and justify any areas where increased funding is needed. Examine the proposed budget for opportunities to shift funds and prioritize funding but keep in mind that contractual obligations come first. With the proposed budget created, the acquisitions librarian should prepare a budget presentation for the library director on the proposed budget including all documentation for the rationale behind any increased funding requests.

An academic budget will typically include categories for serials, standing orders, and firm orders as the programs, and individual resource titles, databases, or departments as the line items. A public library budget may include children's services, youth services, and adult services as program funds with individual service expenditures as line items. An ideal materials budget will be consistent and comprehensive to allow yearly comparisons that provide indicators of what happened in the past as compared to the present and future. Using both line items and programs helps the director, administration, and library board visualize not only the entire budget but gain an understanding of how individual services affect the overall budget. Expenditures are recorded as encumbered when an order is placed and expensed or paid when the item is received and payment is authorized. It is imperative to understand what is both encumbered and expensed otherwise there is a risk of overdrawing the budget. When placing monographic orders, many libraries initially over encumber at list prices, and when books are invoiced at a discount the discounted amounts revert back into the book fund or funds.

A typical budget outline starts with the largest known expenditures for the year. In most cases, this will be serials or continuing resources. If a library receives many of its continuing resources through a consortium, the membership due could be a top expense or priority. Because continuing resources represent contractual ongoing subscriptions, budgeting is based on the previous year's expenditure plus the additional amount calculated from the inflation percentage for the year. Several good sources to use for determining the anticipated inflation rate is Library Journal Periodicals Price Survey published every April, and the *Library Materials Price Index* published in the *Library & Book Trade Almanac.* Cancellations made throughout the previous year should also be factored into the serials budget for the coming year.

Standing orders, approval plans, interlibrary loan expenditures, bindery, and purchase-on-demand expenses may also be factored into a collection budget. Standing orders, like continuing resources, are also contractual agreements, for multi-volume works such as monograph series, collected papers, encyclopedias, or other reference works. As they may or may not be published on a regular schedule, it is often difficult to predict what to allocate. However, a good starting point is tracking the number of volumes issued in the past year to determine an estimated expenditure for the year ahead. If approval plans are used to acquire library materials from a vendor this represents another ongoing commitment that should have a set amount budgeted. The budget for an approval plan should be somewhat predictable as the total amount allocated per vendor is one of the parameter setting options.

Budgeting for firm order purchases is typically last on the list using any remaining funds not budgeted for serials, standing orders, or approval plans. Firm orders are one-time expenditures. In a university library budget, each subject area will have a set amount allocated to a designated fund using an allocation formula that includes data elements such as the number of students enrolled in programs, degrees offered, number of faculty, and cost of materials in each discipline. Public libraries will assign funding for programs, fiction, and nonfiction, as well as audio and visual materials. The firm order budget is the first place to look if requested to reduce or eliminate the budget.

Copyright

Acquisitions professionals will find it useful to have a working knowledge of copyright for licensed or purchased material. In some cases, faculty may have questions or concerns about public performance rights for streaming video, or fair use of DVDs or other library materials for their courses. Copyright law affects policies in other library departments, for example, use policies in access services and reference, and some larger libraries hire librarians with expertise in this area to conduct workshops and review licenses. There are many continuing education resources that are devoted to both copyright and scholarly communications (including Creative Commons licenses), which would benefit both new and experienced acquisitions librarians.

MANAGEMENT OF THE ACQUISITIONS DEPARTMENT

There are two main components of managing an acquisitions department—the staff and the workflow. The new acquisitions librarian should take time to get to know the staff and learn the responsibilities of each staff member. The acquisitions librarian does not need to know each staff member's job intimately, but it's important to have a basic level of understanding of the work that is done (or not done) in the department.

Depending on the size of the library and department, the acquisitions librarian may be responsible for all acquisitions or only a portion of the total. The acquisitions librarian may be a one person show or may have several staff to manage. A list of questions can help in acquiring needed information about the department and workflow.

Questions to Ask

- What responsibilities rest with the acquisitions department?
- Is it only acquisitions of print material?
- Are electronic materials, such as eBooks, included?

- Are serials included?
- Who manages the negotiation and licensing of databases?
- Who is responsible for selecting material or approving purchases?
- Is processing and repair completed in the department?
- Who manages gift acquisitions?
- Does the library have an organizational chart that can be shared with the acquisitions librarian?
- Is there a strategic plan for the library and subsequent goals for technical services and specifically acquisitions? What is the status of progress on established goals?
- When were the policies and workflow documents last updated?

Departmental Organization

It is important to learn the structure of the department. Who does the acquisitions librarian report to? How many staff members are in the department? Do they all report directly to the acquisitions librarian or are there layers to the reporting structure? In many libraries, the acquisitions librarian reports directly to a director or dean and manages all aspects of library acquisitions.

Departmental Priorities and Policies

The acquisitions librarian needs to become familiar with the written policies and workflow documents and learn where they are saved. If there are workflows that are currently not documented, that is a good way to train with a staff member. The documents should also be organized in a way that makes sense and are also easy to access.

Staff Management

It is important to take the time to get to know the staff and the work they do. It may be challenging to be a new manager with staff who have been with the organization for a long time. The acquisitions librarian should go on a fact-finding mission about the work that is done before deciding to make any changes. It may be challenging to introduce new ideas and ways of doing things without getting the buy in from the current staff. There are various ways to get to know the staff and the work they perform, for example, reviewing position descriptions, meeting with members individually, holding staff meetings, establishing workflow studies, scheduling training, and by simply being approachable.

- **Staff meetings:** It is good to get the staff together for regular meetings. An agenda should be set and sent out ahead of time. If staff are required to come with information or are expected to participate in discussion, they should know this ahead of time. The acquisitions librarian should always follow through with any actions that were promised and should follow up with staff who also have action items. Reviewing resources on running effective meetings can be helpful.
- **Be approachable:** The acquisitions librarian should have an open door so any staff member can come and talk about work concerns and issues. The staff member should be welcomed and respected. It is important to address issues as they arise and not let them simmer and fester. It is also a good practice to check-in with staff periodically and not wait for them to approach you. Staff feel that their work is important when the boss takes time to visit with them and ask how their work or day is going. It is also important to let them know that their work is valued, and that the department functions as a team.
- Staff collaboration with other departments: Staff may not realize the impact their work may have on other departments. The acquisitions librarian may want to help facilitate bringing all staff in technical services together to have a common understanding of the work that is done and how the ultimate goal is to serve the library user in a timely manner. Oftentimes when staff across departments come together, workflows can be analyzed and clarified. The work done in the Acquisitions department may intersect with other departments such as cataloging, interlibrary loan, serials, and collection development. It is helpful for everyone in acquisitions to understand how their work fits into the bigger picture of providing resources to the user.

Staff evaluation: How are staff evaluated? Is there a university wide performance program? With an organization wide performance management system, it is important to pay attention to deadlines for staff evaluations and performance reviews. Often there is a mid-year evaluation where the staff member meets with the supervisor and does a self-evaluation. These deadlines should come from the HR department of the organization. The acquisitions librarian needs to get to know the staff evaluation program. Are there classes offered by the HR department on how the staff evaluation system works? Is there another manager in the library who can give an orientation of the system to the new acquisitions librarian? The staff member should never be surprised with a performance evaluation. It is critical that the acquisitions librarian give feedback not just during the evaluation, but also throughout the year.

Most staff evaluations are based on setting goals and documenting progress throughout the year on meeting those goals. If the new acquisitions librarian has never been involved with setting goals, then that will be a skill set that needs to be developed. Goals are typically described as being SMART, which is an acronym for Specific, Measureable, Achievable, Realistic and Trackable. There are many resources available to help develop SMART goals. It is also a good practice to review a staff member's position description once a year, during this performance evaluation for updates or changes in responsibilities, and to tie goals to specific responsibilities outlined in the position description.

Recruiting and Training New Staff

At some point in a manager's career, new staff will need to be hired and trained. Usually a job description will need to be written or revised and posted. Depending on the policies of the library, the acquisitions librarian may be more or less involved in the hiring. At the very least, the acquisitions librarian should be involved in writing the job description. The acquisitions librarian, as the department manager, should also be involved in reviewing resumes, interviewing candidates and selecting a candidate for hire.

Once a new staff member is hired, orientation and training should be provided. The acquisition librarian may conduct the training or delegate someone else do it. It isn't easy to be a good trainer so it's important to make sure the new hire has a chance to practice what is learned and to be given constructive feedback. Training a new hire is also a good time to review workflow documentation and make sure it is up to date.

Communication

Staff need to know what is going on in the department. Communication means sharing of information and this sharing can be done in a number of ways. Information can be shared formally or informally. Common types of communication include email updates, staff meetings, memos, walking or stand-up meetings, and individual meetings. The acquisitions librarian should be clear and direct when communicating with staff. While the performance evaluation period is the formal time to give feedback on a staff member's work, feedback should be given throughout the year. What is important is that staff do not feel left out and surprised when a decision is made. There is no such thing as over communicating. Part of communicating also means listening to the staff. The acquisitions librarian should encourage staff to express ideas, emotions, issues, or concerns. Listening is important.

Management Style

There are plenty of resources to consult about different management styles. The new acquisitions librarian should take the time to figure out the best type of management style to use and realize that different situations may call for different approaches. Different management approaches may also be needed to deal with different staff styles of learning. If the library has a human resources department, they may offer training for new managers.

COLLABORATION WITH OTHER DEPARTMENTS WITHIN THE LIBRARY

Collection Development

The first order of business is to find out who the collection development librarians are in your library and how they are organized. Are they called collection development librarians, collection managers, subject librarians, or something else? Is there a separate department that only does collection development? Are the reference librarians also subject selectors and therefore only devote a small amount of time to collection development? Is there a team or group of librarians that meet regularly to discuss collection development? How have the librarians with collection responsibility interacted with the acquisitions librarian in the past?

It is vitally important that the acquisitions librarian work closely with the collection development librarians in order to manage and spend the materials budget in a responsible and timely manner. It is also important for the acquisitions librarian to manage the workflow that comes from the collection development librarians so that the acquisitions and cataloging staff have a steady flow of material instead of peaks and valleys with the peaks being at the end of the fiscal year. Establishing spending deadlines with the collection development librarians work to ensure even spending over the year. The acquisitions librarian should plan to attend meetings with collection development librarians to serve as a resource to answer any questions concerning fund balances.

In working with others in the library, an acquisitions manager has an opportunity and perhaps even the responsibility of supplying other librarians and staff with information on ordering, allocations, and expenditures. The acquisitions librarian should serve as the expert on the vendor ordering system and provide training to others tasked with placing orders. The acquisitions librarian should also be able to answer questions about the budget. A knowledge of how funds are allocated and who is given responsibility for placing orders is essential.

The acquisitions librarian sets deadlines for better management of workflow throughout the year. Fiscal years run either January–December, or more common in academic libraries, July 1–June 30.

For example, collection managers may be asked to spend 50 percent of their firm order budget by September 1, 75 percent by the end of December, and 100 percent by the end of February. If they don't follow these deadlines, then there is the chance the money not spent will be pooled for the collection management team to decide to purchase other needed materials. It is preferred to spend remaining balances on one-time purchases instead of continuing resources that result in ongoing expenditures. An example of a one-time expenditure might be a newspaper archive or front list of eBooks by a publisher.

In addition, the acquisition librarian also provides a monthly status of the book funds for the collection managers. These reports should be easy to understand. Acquisitions librarians are also in a position to coordinate publisher and vendor meetings and training for all librarians and staff. The most important point to remember is the acquisitions librarian is a partner with the collection development and electronic resources librarians in spending the budget in a responsible manner.

Electronic Resources

If you work in a library with an electronic resources librarian, it is important to determine who handles the licensing and acquisition of electronic resources. In most cases, the electronic resources librarian will manage trials, negotiate pricing, and handle renewals with the acquisitions librarian responsible for creating the purchase order and ensuring payment. In other libraries, the acquisitions librarian manages all aspects of acquiring and renewing electronic resources. Some campus policies may also require the person who signs the license to approve the renewal of a resource. Some institutions may require licenses to be signed by a procurement and contracts office.

Cataloging

The cataloging and acquisitions department will work closely together as acquisitions of materials and cataloging for discovery are interdependent. Both units share the goal to make material available to the users in a timely and efficient manner. It is therefore important to establish a good working relationship with the head of cataloging. Establishing periodic meetings is one way to ensure good communication between units, discuss projects, and review and revise workflow as needed. There are many tasks that acquisitions staff can take on that will expedite cataloging. For example, acquisitions staff might be involved in rapid cataloging for shelf-ready approvals and firm orders. As part of the ordering process, acquisitions staff routinely download new MARC records from OCLC or other sources. If a staff member is responsible for receiving new material in the Acquisitions module, this person's duties can be expanded to include doing rapid cataloging using a checklist that is developed by the cataloging department. If the title passes the checklist an item can be created, and the title can go directly to the circulation department for shelving. If the title does not pass the checklist, it is routed to cataloging. Acquisitions staff may also be tasked with deleting records for lost books that are not being replaced. In some libraries, the acquisitions department is responsible for maintaining electronic standing orders or may work with cataloging to manage MARC records for new electronic resources. When new titles are available, the cataloging department needs to be notified of new marc records and other information needed to catalog the resource. A spreadsheet can be created using a shared system such as Google docs, to keep track of these resources. The acquisitions librarian can enter the information that a new title is available to alert the cataloging department.

Interlibrary Loan

The acquisitions librarian may work collaboratively with interlibrary loan (ILL) when budgeting, for a patron driven acquisition program, or for collection development purposes. ILL is able to produce statistics to aid in acquisitions, collection development, and serial evaluations.

Library Reserves

In an academic library, the acquisitions librarian may work with the reserves department to purchase course material to support academic programs. For some libraries, the reserves department may ask the acquisitions department to purchase multiple copies of high use texts. If eBooks with unlimited users are requested, the budget may need to be closely monitored in order to not exceed available funds.

Questions about Orders

The acquisitions librarian serves as an important resource in the acquisition of materials and especially in determining where an item is in the ordering process. If the title is ordered through the book ordering system (GOBI Library Solutions or OASIS) the acquisition librarian can look into the appropriate system to see if the title has been shipped. The acquisition or cataloging module of the ILS can also indicate who touched the book last to identify where the item may be located.

CHAPTER **TWO**

Standards and Best Practices for Acquisitions

Acquisitions involves use of standard procedures and best practices. This chapter provides a brief overview of some of the standard procedures or best practices likely to be encountered. While the literature may indicate some disagreement over the existence of professional standards for acquisitions, the Association for Library Collections and Technical Services (ALCTS) developed a statement of principles and standards of acquisition practice that should be adopted by anyone involved in acquisitions work:

> Gives first consideration to the missions, objectives and policies of their institution; strives to ensure good stewardship and maximum value of the institution's resources; regards each transaction on its own merits and grants all competing vendors equal consideration insofar as the established policies of their library permit; conducts all dealings according to fair, ethical, and legal business practices and fosters such conduct

in others; declines gifts or other arrangements that may result, or be perceived to result, in personal gain or inappropriately influence decisions; observes intellectual property rights and freedom of information/protection of privacy rights and responsibilities, including contractual confidentiality requirements; accords a prompt and courteous reception to all who call on legitimate business and communicates the institution's interests honestly; strives to stay informed and knowledgeable of industry trends and current practices; strives to develop and use practical and efficient methods for the conduct of their responsibilities while incorporating sound fiscal practices; counsels and assists colleagues and fellow acquisitions professionals regarding acquisitions principles and practices, in service to the profession.

Developed by the ALCTS Education Task Force; endorsed by the ALCTS Acquisitions Section and adopted by the ALCTS Board of Directors, Midwinter Meeting, January 25, 2019

STANDARD PROCEDURES FOR ORDERING

1. *Check to make sure the library does not already have the item:* This can coincide with the creation of the purchase order (PO), since the creation of the PO in many ordering systems often requires a catalog record. Even though the requestor may say he or she checked the catalog, it is always a good idea to have the acquisitions staff verify that the item is not already owned or accessible. Some ordering systems may require or offer this type of verification. If the item is owned, acquisitions staff should communicate this to the requestor and see if there are additional instructions.
2. *Creating the purchase order:* Many integrated library systems (ILS) or vendor ordering systems will create the PO automatically. To create the purchase order, a record needs to be in the catalog. Acquisitions departments usually download records from OCLC, or create a dummy record (that will later be edited or overlaid by the cataloging department), or import a file with records from a vendor. Once the record is in the

catalog, the purchase order can be created. Purchase orders may require the fund code (see navigating the ILS system for more information on fund codes) for the order, the vendor, and other information depending on the needs of a specific library or ordering system.

3. *Placing the order:* There are several ways an order for an item can be placed. Typically, orders are placed through a vendor ordering system or an online site like Amazon, but orders may also be placed directly with a publisher by email, fax, or telephone. Depending on how the order is received, the acquisitions staff may want to check a few different vendors to get the lowest price. Many libraries use at least one monograph vendor, such as GOBI Library Solutions, but may supplement purchases with another seller like Amazon.

4. *When the order arrives, there should be an established process to receive the orders.* To ensure a proper check and balance, the person who receives and verifies shipments should be different from the person who places the orders. For each shipment of materials, the items are unpacked, and each item is checked against a packing slip or invoice. The item can then be matched with internal paperwork or system notes. Check-in can also involve catching vendor errors such as sending the wrong book or a duplicate copy. Often times, the internal paperwork or system notes will have instructions for cataloging or requestor notification. Once through the receiving process, the items are checked for defects and then sent to cataloging.

It is essential to review each received item for defects or damage in order to expedite the return of items with errors. Most vendors will allow items to be returned when problems are detected. A quality check typically involves thumbing through the volume to check for correct pagination, and to note any physical defects. Some things to watch for include pages without text, pages stuck together, mistakes in page numbering, or pages not bound well. Items that do not pass the manual review check are returned to the vendor. DVDs are typically checked during the cataloging process but can be visually scanned during the check-in process to ensure the DVD is not broken and that the title on the DVD matches the title on the case.

An example of a more thorough quality check is when the acquisitions department handles shelf-ready titles. Shelf-ready means the item will arrive with a certain level of pre-processing completed by the vendor. Depending on the acquisitions workflow, these items may come with OCLC records to overlay the provisional record that was downloaded or created at the time of the order. Some acquisitions departments will handle the initial check of these titles and then route the title to cataloging if it needs more work or send it directly to the circulation department if it passes the quality check. Some areas that are commonly checked include: pre-processing done on the item such as bookplate in the proper place and not covering up information, library stamp, barcode affixed, and call number label correct. If the item is being checked against the OCLC record, some fields to check include title page, author, OCLC number, ISBN, publisher, pagination.

BEST PRACTICES FOR
Gift Funds/Development Funds

Some libraries may have a development or gift monetary fund and the acquisitions librarian may be tasked with monitoring the balances and reporting those balances to collection managers or library administration. Some funds may restrict how the money can be used. It is important to get the written description of each fund and who can make the decision about using the money. Do the collection managers or team have the authority to decide how the money is spent? Do the collection librarians make a recommendation to the library director?

Once the decision is made to utilize gift funds, this money needs to be tracked in the ILS. To not track it gives a false impression of how much money was spent acquiring resources. A separate spreadsheet can be kept to tracks the funds. At the end of the fiscal year, the acquisitions librarian can prepare a report for the library administration on the gift funds that were used and the resources that were purchased with those funds.

Another similar program is cost sharing resources between an academic library and other departments across the campus.

If another department or school pays for part of a resource that is managed by the library, the flow of money from the school or department needs to be tracked. The tracking is similar to gift or development funds, and a PO may be established with a generic title, for example, University Funds. Once the transfer is processed, the paperwork is sent to the acquisition librarian. An invoice is then created against the PO to show the inflow of money to the ledger, and then the money is transferred to the proper fund code where the resource is purchased. Another spreadsheet tracks these cost shares. This ensures an easy way to see which departments have paid their portion and which departments need to be reminded.

It is important to have a memo of understanding (MOU) with the cost sharing unit. If the other unit no longer wants to pay their share of the cost, what will the library do? Cancel the resource? Pick up the full cost of the resource? Before any cost-sharing arrangement is set up, all parties involved should agree to the terms and decide how to proceed when one party wants to cancel the arrangement.

Gift Books and Donations

In many libraries, the acquisitions department coordinates the workflow of gifts and donations of books and other materials. On the surface, handling book donations would appear to be an easy process, but the workflow, policies, and processing can be somewhat time consuming and complicated. Gift books can come from many sources including other libraries, estates, faculty members, library staff, publishers, organizations, and individual community donors. Some libraries do not accept donations due to staffing demands or space constraints. Other libraries may only accept certain types of donations, depending on the library gift policy. Libraries may have a friends group handle all donations.

Once acquired, libraries may add gifts to the collection, replace library copies with gift copies if the gift is in better condition, or sell the books in a book sale or through a book dealer. Regardless of how a library handles donations, a new acquisitions librarian should be familiar with the process and determine their roles, if any, regarding gifts and donations. If the role is significant, the acquisitions librarian may need to effectively interact with donors (and possibly a friends group), learn the appropriate workflow, and become familiar with the library's gifts policy and processes for managing gifts.

A policy outlining the acceptance of gifts is essential. A gifts policy should reflect the needs of the library and serve as a useful and consistent point of reference for librarians and staff coordinating donations. The library's gift policy should specifically address the types of materials accepted or excluded and stipulate that materials should be in good condition. For example, many libraries do not accept print periodicals, with the possible exception of filling gaps from missing issues. The policy should also outline what happens to donated items and offer the donor the option to have materials returned if not added to the collection. Procedures for donating materials should include instructions on where to drop off donations, who to contact if there are questions, and completion of the donor agreement form. It is important to clarify the procedures as some donors may request library staff to visit their homes to pick up large donations of books. The library's gift policy should also mention how donations are acknowledged. Libraries typically do not have the staffing to record each title donated, but many libraries will count and record the number of titles donated.

Donors usually expect some level of recognition and thanks for donating to the library. Faculty, staff, and alumni often have deep ties to a college or university, and donating to the library can be way of expressing gratitude and loyalty to their educational institution. Members of the community not affiliated with the college or university will also expect donations to be recognized. A thank-you letter acknowledging the gift, signed by a library administrator, should be sent as part of the donations process. Donors managing a relative's estate may ask for memorial bookplates for titles added to the collection. The library should determine if it will add bookplates if requested. Some libraries offer electronic book plating which involves a notation in the catalog record.

Interacting and communicating effectively with donors is perhaps the most important aspect of the gifts process. It is very important for librarians accepting gifts to be cognizant of the feelings of the donor. Donors may wish to spend a few minutes talking to the acquisitions librarian or staff member accepting the gift and taking the time to welcome and thank the donor is an important aspect of the gifts and donation process. Even if a collection is not accepted, potential donors should have a positive experience and feel that the library was at least grateful for their offer. Donors often call unexpectedly or visit the library without making an appointment. The nature of acquisitions work is demanding, and the librarian may be in the middle of a project. Acquisitions librarians responsible for coordinating donations should anticipate these interruptions, and plan to take a few minutes to interact with potential donors tactfully and cordially. The intrinsic reward can be a nice gift for the collection, simply for spending a few minutes speaking with a donor.

Many donors have certain expectations regarding their gifts and the donation process, and transparency, clear communication, and written policy and procedures are essential for avoiding any problems and misunderstandings regarding donations. For example, some donors may expect all of their books and materials, regardless of condition or age, to be added to the library collection. However, unless a donation is of particular value or has historical significance or unique subject coverage, most general donations will contain at least some items, or perhaps a majority, not meeting the criteria for addition to the library collection. Depending on the gifts policy of the library, these books could be sold at an annual library book sale, discarded, or donated to another non-profit entity in the community. The acquisitions librarian should clearly communicate to the donor what will become of the gift books, if donated. In some cases, a donor may withdraw the offer if the books are not added to the library collection. Many donors also feel that their books are valuable or rare, and some will expect the library to appraise their gift books. Many libraries include a statement about appraisals in their gift policy and simply do not offer this service. State laws may prohibit such appraisals, and most libraries do not have a method or staff with the appropriate background to offer accurate appraisals for books.

Acquisitions librarians working with book donations may also be responsible for coordinating annual book sales, especially in smaller academic libraries. Book sales require a lot of work, but offer an important library service for students, other library constituents, and the community. Depending on the library, a friends of the library group may play an active role in the annual sale, or even take on most of the responsibility for a sale (at some larger academic libraries, friends groups may exclusively manage the majority of book donations and the annual sales). Librarians new to acquisitions may wish to attend friends of the library meetings and get to know the members. The members of friends groups may volunteer to staff the sale or to volunteer throughout the year to prepare for an annual sale. Preparing for a sale can be time consuming, and drawing on volunteers is essential for a successful sale. Ideally, books donated for the sale should be arranged by subject category or genre, and books in poor condition weeded out prior to the sale. In addition, books will need to be priced and labeled, although some libraries charge one standard price for paperbacks or cloth books. Some of the nicer books and sets may need to be priced separately. A library may also sell music, DVDs, and materials in other formats, and these items will require a separate section during the sale. Signage is important, and promoting the sale in advance on social media, the library's website, and local news outlets is essential for a successful sale. Moving the books to the sale site and arranging them on shelves or tables depending on the number of books, can also take time and require more volunteers.

Publisher/Vendor Relations

Working with publishers and vendors is a large part of acquisitions work so establishing relationships with reps is an important and required task. You will work with vendors and publishers to establish and renew subscriptions, request discounts, negotiate pricing, set up trials, place orders, process licenses and invoices, return items, access MARC records, schedule training, obtain use statistics, and troubleshoot problems. Collection development or electronic resources librarians may also be involved in working directly with vendors. You may also be responsible for monitoring the performance of your vendors.

To begin, find out which publishers and vendors your library has active accounts with along with the names of customer and sales representatives. Reach out to the vendor representatives to introduce yourself, schedule a visit, and inquire about new services or training. Publishers and vendors are constantly in flux and some vendors, like EBSCO or ProQuest, may have multiple reps for different services, such as discovery, monographs, serials, databases, technical support, and payments. It may be helpful to establish a spreadsheet for publishers/vendors listing the reps and contact information. Also, take time to educate the publisher or vendor about your library organization. In some libraries, the person who initiates the order may be different from the person who makes the purchase decision or handles licenses.

Library service vendors work with publishers to purchase monograph titles at a volume discount and then resell the books to libraries for a discounted price based on the individual library/vendor arrangement. Historically, only large firm order suppliers had inventory warehouses full of titles waiting to ship. They generally made the most popular titles available immediately and waited for a sufficient number of requests before ordering from the publisher.

Acquisitions librarians may also be tasked with monitoring the health of a vendor or evaluating a new vendor. When evaluating a new vendor or assessing the health of an existing monograph vendor it may be helpful to establish a checklist of things to consider. Such a checklist could include:

- Ordering system—easy to search, navigate, use to place orders, integrates with existing ILS
- Quantity of monographs in stock
- eBook purchase options-may require establishing separate contracts with publishers/vendors
- Shipping costs
- Delivery time
- Binding and costs for binding—ask for a price list of services
- Returns policies
- Customer service and technical support
- Shelf-ready services
- MARC records
- Payment options

It is also important in monitoring the health of the vendor to regularly review trade journals, lists, and blogs for information specific to the vendors you use. Vendors want feedback—no matter how critical—so do not be shy about telling them when things are not working and why. Find out how and with whom to report problems. Do you report problems to your sales rep, to a customer service rep or to a technical support rep? Keep a record of all communication about the issue including response dates and the final resolution.

eBook Acquisitions

Acquisitions librarians may play a role in managing eBook acquisitions, in addition to acquiring books in print format. Acquiring and managing eBooks can be somewhat complicated, largely because of the various acquisition models, the licensing, the sheer number of publishers and vendors selling eBooks, pricing considerations, and a number of other important questions to consider prior to making a purchase. Multiple purchase options exist such as subscription to a collection or vendor package, a one-time purchase, or demand driven purchases. Many libraries employ all three options. The acquisitions librarian may find it helpful to develop an informal checklist of purchase considerations, to guide the acquisition of eBooks.

With so many vendors and publishers offering eBooks, duplication is certainly an important factor to consider. Many eBook subscriptions offered through publishers and vendors contain significant overlap. Some libraries may decide to purchase subject collections that contain some overlap to ensure permanent access to these titles. Duplication with print can also be a consideration. In cases of print and electronic, both may be acceptable, especially when print is the requested format by patrons.

Costs and availability of titles will also drive purchase decisions. In some cases, it may be more cost-effective to obtain eBooks through a vendor subscription package or consortium instead of directly from the publisher. Some libraries may stipulate that eBook content is Digital Rights Management (DRM) free, which allows access to unlimited simultaneous users, and unlimited printing, copying, and downloading. It is also important to inquire about MARC records and work with the library's cataloging unit to manage the MARC records. New acquisitions librarians purchasing and managing eBooks will need to familiarize themselves with various acquisition models and determine which of these purchase options best serve the needs of their library.

Many publishers and vendors offer libraries the option of acquiring subject or interdisciplinary eBook collections as either a subscription or a one-time purchase. The main advantage of acquiring an eBook collection on subscription is the cost, which typically is much less than purchasing the collection, at least in the short term. Because eBook titles offered through a subscription are leased, they may disappear if a publisher later pulls the titles from the subscription. However, a subscription may provide the library with more time to evaluate the platform, obtain usage data, and determine if the content meets the needs of the user community. When evaluating an eBook collection purchase versus a subscription, ask for the cost difference, if there is a platform fee, and the list of titles included in the purchase versus the subscription.

A subscription may not offer as many current titles as the eBook collection purchase, but it may offer the advantage of updates. eBook subscriptions will require more MARC record maintenance (especially for large interdisciplinary collections containing titles from many publishers) since titles are added and deleted monthly. For those libraries interested in collecting eBooks to preserve the scholarly monograph and enhance their collections, the disadvantage of a subscription is that eBooks are leased and not permanently acquired. A one-time purchase of an eBook collection can be a good way to spend end-of-year balances. A new acquisitions librarian, in consultation with the library administration and subject librarians, should evaluate the needs of the library to determine if a subscription is the best option. The library's annual budget, use metrics, the information needs of library stakeholders, and the long-term goals of the library all may need to be carefully considered.

Almost all of the major STEM publishers, and many humanities and social sciences publishers, allow libraries to buy front list collections for a specific discipline or disciplines, as well as subject-specific backlist titles. Although these collections may be expensive, depending on the number purchased, buying an entire collection usually results in a discounted price per title which can make the collections attractive to purchase. Increasingly, the major publishers in the sciences are offering these collections DRM free, offering a further incentive to purchase these subject collections, or even the entire suite of subject collections from the publisher. In addition, many publishers participate in long-term preservation projects, like Portico and LOCKSS, essentially guaranteeing access to the eBooks perpetually. These one-time purchases allow academic libraries to build substantial scholarly eBooks collections in certain subject disciplines with owned rather than leased titles. Major publishers in the humanities and social sciences are following suit, offering comprehensive or subject-specific collections in an array of disciplines, allowing libraries to offer exceptionally rich eBook content to constituents. An advantage to a one-time eBook package is less maintenance with MARC records. One disadvantage for acquiring these permanent collections can be the cost, and a library will need to make a budget commitment year after year to acquire these front list collections. Some libraries may decide to subscribe to some collections while purchasing others, depending on the needs of the library. As previously mentioned, these one-time purchases are a good way to expend year-end balances so it may be useful to keep a running list of desired packages to evaluate for purchase throughout the year.

Acquisitions librarians can also purchase eBooks individually (ala carte), selecting them on a title-by-title basis. The major library service vendors offer the option to purchase single eBook titles in their bibliographic databases (for example, GOBI Library Solutions and OASIS). Titles may also be purchased directly from publishers. The chief disadvantage of purchasing eBooks as single titles consists of paying a relatively higher cost for each title (compared to discounted eBook subject packages). Single eBook purchases are usually more expensive than the print version and may come without a discount; whereas the same titles in print purchased through a library vendor are usually discounted (the amount depends on the service agreement with the library). Also, a library may pay additional costs to increase the number of simultaneous users for a particular title (a form of DRM), and some publishers and vendors can charge substantially more than the print version for certain reference works or other specialty titles. License agreements for the publishers will need to be in place to purchase titles individually in the bibliographic databases (although license agreements are required for subject eBooks collections as well). The time spent selecting and acquiring each title is perhaps another disadvantage, compared to buying large collections of titles preselected by the vendor or the publisher. However, some libraries may find that it makes sense to select eBooks individually in order to add current front list content not covered in subscriptions, or otherwise not purchased in various subject collections. Single title selections will also provide new acquisitions librarians with the flexibility to purchase individual requests for eBooks, and the option to make targeted purchases from a variety of publishers without having to acquire the entire collection from a publisher.

As with other electronic resources, new acquisitions librarians may need to play a role in the licensing process. At some academic libraries, particularly at smaller institutions, the acquisitions librarian may serve as the point person for pricing and licensing negations with an eBook vendor. New acquisitions librarians will need to familiarize themselves with DRM and pay particular attention to DRM provisions in license agreements. Of course normal copyright restrictions will still apply, but DRM free collections offer the most flexibility for patrons. Some eBook collections may simply not be available without some level of DRM, but a provision like ILL, may possibly be open to negotiation. At a minimum, an eBook collection should at least be available both on and off campus to patrons, and ideally, books should also be accessible simultaneously to multiple patrons. Many collections will come with hosting fees, although these fees can sometimes be waived for the first year, or possibly reduced through negotiation. New acquisitions librarians need to understand the licensing policies in place at their institution and to carefully follow the licensing procedures. Many colleges and universities require authorized personnel such as an administrator in the budgeting office, to review and sign an agreement before a purchase is finalized. Acquisitions librarians should work carefully with vendors to make sure price quotes and negotiated changes to licenses appear in writing, and that the vendor understands that an eBook collection purchase is not guaranteed until the license is vetted and preapproved according to policies in place at their institution.

Acquisitions librarians should also check to ensure that MARC records are available and come at no additional cost when acquiring an eBook collection. Depending on the library, the acquisitions librarian may coordinate or participate at least to some degree in the MARC management process, which is an essential for providing access to a newly acquired collection. MARC records typically appear in the administrative portal of the eBook platform when the collection is activated for a library, which usually occurs about the time the product is invoiced. MARC records are downloaded into the ILS using MarcEdit or another MARC editing application in order to appear in the library's catalog and discovery service. MARC records, depending on the collection, may also be accessible from OCLC, or possibly be automatically loaded in a holdings management service provided by a vendor like EBSCO. If loaded locally, the acquisitions librarian may need to work with their systems or cataloging department to ensure that records for collections appear in the catalog or discovery service. The acquisitions librarian should receive the login credentials for the administrative portal, and establish or share administrative privileges for a cataloging, systems, or electronic services librarian. A schedule may need to be established to load regular add and delete files, which are configured to include proxy links and possibly item categories to provide bibliographic control of the records (for removal, if needed). Regardless of the level of participation in MARC management, the acquisitions librarian should always follow up to make sure MARC records are in place and discoverable for all eBook acquisitions.

In addition to MARC management, the administrative portal for an eBook platform serves other useful functions for acquisitions librarians. The portal allows librarians to run use statistics reports, which are useful for completing the collections portion of the ACRL Academic Library Trends and Statistics Survey (and IPEDS Academic Libraries component) and other possible surveys. Many eBook platforms provide statistical COUNTER compliant reports to evaluate use, and some platforms provide other custom reports that may contain useful information (pricing, number of turn ways, and other use metrics). The administrative eBook portal allows acquisitions librarians to effectively manage and evaluate eBook resources. Acquisitions librarians new to the position should know how to generate eBook statistics, which are also useful for making decisions regarding cancellations or future purchases. Most vendor reports can be exported and saved. The administrative portal may also allow librarians to purchase single titles from a vendor (or possibly upgrade a title for additional users). Some platforms offer the library branding capabilities, and administrators can also adjust other configurations (for example, restricting viewable access to purchased content only), universally applying the proxy to persistent links, and turning on or off undesired features in the database.

Pricing for eBooks is always an important consideration, and acquisitions librarians should check to see if any consortia discounts apply. Negotiations with publishers to lower prices or to waive hosting and access fees should be requested before finalizing any agreement to purchase eBook content. In addition, acquisitions librarians should take advantage of recording and tracking subscription and package eBook acquisitions in a library's electronic resources management (ERM) service, if one is available. Acquisitions librarians may also be responsible for promoting collections or for supplying information to colleagues in the library to promote new acquisitions. Public and academic librarians can promote collections through social media, newsletters, and their other forms of library communication.

Acquisition of Textbook Alternatives

Many colleges and universities are now encouraging faculty to explore options for using materials and textbooks resulting in monetary savings or zero costs for their students. Acquisitions librarians may work at institutions with faculty who request the library to purchase electronic versions of textbooks and other assigned books to support their classes. Books may be available in DRM (Digital Rights Management) free eBook collections, like *Books at JSTOR*, or through a la carte purchases from vendors or publishers. Some libraries may also proactively promote OER (Open Educational Resources) materials to faculty. Open collections are free, and by definition, these eBooks and other course material are openly available to faculty and students regardless of any mediation by the library. These resources typically have a Creative Commons license. Some libraries pay membership fees to support OER with organizations like SPARC or Knowledge Unlatched. Supporting and providing access to open resources is an important and ongoing conversation in scholarly communications, and acquisitions librarians involved in acquiring textbooks or other required books for classes should be familiar with this topic.

Demand-Driven Acquisitions (DDA)/ Evidence-Based Acquisitions (EBA)

Demand-driven (DDA) or patron-driven acquisitions (PDA) has become a standard acquisitions model used by numerous academic libraries. The concept of the DDA model is fairly straight forward, though designing and managing demand driven acquisitions can be quite complicated. DDA consists of populating the library catalog with MARC records from a vendor or publisher (or sometimes more than a single vendor or publisher) for eBooks not owned by the library. The pool of MARC records, called a consideration pool, is selected by the library according to subject, date, price and publisher parameters (the latter when a vendor offers holdings from multiple publishers). The consideration pool can vary in size from perhaps a few hundred initial titles to tens of thousands depending on the library and the scope of the DDA service. Additional MARC records are added to the pool (downloaded by the library) as new titles are published and become available through the vendor or publisher. Pricing for the DDA often involves an upfront fee and possibly a platform fee. Once the DDA is established, individual titles are purchased after a short-term loan (STL) is triggered by a patron. Depending on the pricing model, libraries may pay a certain percentage of the eBook list price for each STL (a book must actually be used for a certain number of minutes or other activity, like printing, to count as an STL trigger). A library will usually set up the DDA service to automatically purchase a title after a certain number of triggers, for example, three or four triggers (or STLs) would result in an automatic purchase. The list price is paid for an automatic purchase, in addition to costs associated with the short-term loans. Libraries might opt for a "pay as you go" invoicing workflow or use a deposit account with the publisher or vendor.

Evidence-based acquisitions, offered by many publishers and vendors, allows libraries access to an entire collection (such as a specific subject collection or designated years of front list or backlist titles). With an evidence-based acquisitions program, the library pays the vendor a specified amount up front. For example, a library might pay $5,000 to have one year's access to $50,000 worth of eBook titles. At the end of the term, the library will select $5,000 worth of titles to acquire based on usage. JSTOR, Project Muse, SAGE, and other major publishers offer EBA to academic libraries.

Most of the major publishers and vendors now offer some form of demand-driven acquisitions for books and streaming films, and publishers are increasingly offering eBooks using the EBA model. These acquisition models continue to change and evolve, and many vendors and publishers offer webinars with current information regarding these programs for libraries.

The great advantage of DDA is that a library only pays for the eBooks that receive use. In addition, patrons have access (depending on the size of the consideration pool) to vast numbers of eBooks that a library is not required to initially purchase and possibly could not afford to purchase. A disadvantage consists of the time commitment needed to effectively manage the MARC records and other DDA related workflow. Large amounts of MARC records may need to be downloaded into the ILS, or possibly removed. Some libraries participate in DDA programs managed largely by a library consortium, or possibly a library services vendor to mitigate some of the time commitment. Fluctuating budgets may also pose a problem, and a library may find it necessary to pause or discontinue DDA due to cost or budget issues. Philosophically, some librarians feel that DDA (since the patron essentially functions as the selector for the short-term needs of a particular research project) may not be the best method to develop a comprehensive library collection.[1] Relying solely on DDA, a library might miss certain important scholarly works, thus undermining the preservation of the "scholarly record... for future generations."[2] Librarians implementing demand-driven acquisitions should strike a balance between the short-term needs of library patrons with long-term collection development goals. New acquisitions librarians may wish to carefully consider a number of questions prior to designing or implementing DDA project.

- How much money can the library afford to budget for DDA?
- Will the DDA service support a certain program, meet some other specific need, or will the service be interdisciplinary and comprehensive?
- Will the library select a certain publisher (for example, a specialty publisher) or choose an aggregate vendor?
- Would evidence-based acquisitions (EBA) better serve the library than traditional DDA?
- How will the MARC records be managed?

- Will the library place a deposit with the vendor or publisher, or pay each invoice on a weekly or monthly schedule?
- Does a local library consortium offer DDA, or does the library's primary book services vendor offer a DDA management program, and at what cost?

Many books and research articles are available on the topic of demand-driven acquisitions. The *NISO Demand Driven Acquisition of Monographs,* published in 2014, offers a good starting point for new acquisitions librarians interested in learning more about DDA.[3]

Interlibrary Loan

Many libraries have a program where materials requested through interlibrary loan (ILL) are purchased instead of borrowed if they meet set criteria. Typical criteria include cost to purchase requested item, date of publication, and relevance to the primary user community. There is an expectation that titles that are ordered for ILL are ready for the patron within forty-eight hours of arriving in the library (regular working hours, M–F, 9–5). This usually means the title is rush ordered and then fast cataloged when it arrives. There are many articles in the literature that talk about patron-driven acquisitions and using ILL data for purchase decisions and further reading on this practice is encouraged.

Approval Plans

Many libraries use approval plans to acquire books and other materials, and in large libraries, approval plans may be the central method for library acquisitions. In an approval plan, newly published books are automatically shipped to a library, according to the library's preapproved subject profiles, with the option of keeping or returning titles.[4] An approval plan helps to ensure that a library does not inadvertently miss important titles for the collection. Librarians new to acquisitions should understand how an approval plan works. Library approval plans, initially referred to as "gathering plans" or "blanket order plans", started after the Second World War when books were sometimes hard to acquire.[5] Academic libraries still use blanket order plans, but unlike an approval plan, a library may not be able to return titles.[6] A number of vendors offer blanket order plans in foreign languages or other specialized areas, which can be used to enhance a library's holdings.[7] Specialized blanket order plans may be used alongside a library's regular approval plan.

An approval plan is typically set up with a major library services vendor, although vendors that specialize in certain materials, like music or books published in other countries, may also offer approval plans to libraries. Approval plans require working with the vendor to establish a customized profile based on collection needs and available funds. The specifications for keeping or returning items sent on approval will be outlined in the library's contract with the vendor. Often the library may be required to pay shipping for returned items sent through an approval plan. In academic libraries, subject librarians may look at the books and make decisions regarding titles to keep from new shipments of approval books.[8] In large public library systems, children's librarians may review and select from picture books sent on approval. It is also quite possible that some libraries may simply add titles received on approval (unless damaged) with very limited levels of review. Depending on the library's approval plan, librarians may also make decisions regarding the acquisition of eBook titles profiled in a vendor's collection development database, for example, in GOBI.[9] Larger research and public libraries may have approval plans in place with more than one vendor.

Approval plans offer a number of advantages for libraries. For larger academic libraries that collect comprehensively, approval plans can reduce the need for subject librarians to review and select large numbers of individual titles, and subsequently save library staff time.[10] The plans also provide timely access for newly published items without having to rely or wait on a book review.[11] Libraries often receive discounts for approval books depending on negotiations with the vendor. For example, a library may agree to spend a certain amount based on annual spending projections in order to receive a specified discount from the vendor. Approval plans help with budget management by allowing the library to expend funds at a predictable rate throughout the fiscal year.[12] Specific publishers or subject areas can be added or eliminated from a plan, and the plan can be stopped and restarted in the event of a budget cut or spending freeze.

An approval plan may already be in place or a new acquisitions librarian may need to set up an entirely new plan. Setting up an approval plan starts with selecting a library services vendor. A number of factors may be considered, including pricing, invoicing and payment methods, historical reputation of the vendor, consortium considerations (if other libraries in a consortium or state primarily use the same vendor), and ability to meet the specialized or comprehensive collection development needs of the library. Considerations might also include the different levels of technical specifications available and other services offered, for example, EDI ordering (electronic data interchange), automated MARC delivery, technical assistance, training for subject librarians, and shelf-ready services. A vendor should also provide a high level of customer service, be flexible enough to tailor an approval plan specifically to the local needs of the library (in terms of coverage and technical specifications), and accommodate any possible future changes to the plan.

Once a vendor is selected, the next step is to develop an approval plan profile. Approval plans are customized to meet the exact subject strengths and collection needs of a library. Subject or collection librarians may also be involved in establishing approval plan profiles. A profile determines which titles are sent on approval to the library and can be based on academic subjects, reading and content levels, price, format (print, cloth, or electronic), publisher, geographic location, language, awards, and other parameters. Approval plans are set up and managed electronically, using the vendor's bibliographic database. A vendor may provide a highly detailed spreadsheet or form listing the subject profiles available for selection (possibly arranged by LC Classification), for the library to complete, and often offer assistance in establishing the profiles. The library can then choose to have books automatically shipped on approval for certain subject areas and block other subjects to prevent shipping. A library can also arrange to receive electronic slips for certain subject profiles in lieu of the actual books, which is known as a slip plan. After the approval plan is in place, books meeting the profile criteria will periodically ship to the library (or will become available to preview in eBook format, as mentioned above).

At some institutions, faculty from various departments may provide input for a library's approval plan. Adjustments to a plan may correspond to new academic programs or the elimination of certain programs. Budget considerations will also play a role and may determine how open or narrow an approval plan is for a particular library. Large research libraries usually collect extensively and may also complement approvals with firm order selections from electronic slips. In smaller university and college libraries, where budgets may preclude an approval plan, libraries may rely exclusively on reviewing and selecting titles from slips rather than having books shipped automatically.[13]

Slips allow subject librarians to purchase newly published titles on a selective basis. In the past, libraries were sent actual paper slips for new titles, but now most vendors use electronic slips delivered through their bibliographic databases. Electronic slips contain standard bibliographic data, including the author, title, subject, publisher, price, and publication year. Additional information on a slip might include the audience level, the publication type, series (if applicable), the discount, availability, table of contents, or other information about the author or title. Some libraries may subscribe to additional features, such as full textbook reviews, or have access to the purchasing history of the title from other libraries. In a slip plan, subject librarians are usually notified when slips from newly published titles in their areas become available. Slips may be searched by author, title, subject, key terms, or by LC class, and in some cases, even by fund code. Titles selected from slips are ordered directly from the vendor's bibliographic database.

An approval or slip plan will also require setting up the technical specifications for managing the acquisitions workflow. Books shipped on approval will still require the creation of purchase orders and invoices in the local ILS. Many academic libraries design the workflow to batch the download of MARC records into the ILS with order information to automatically create purchase orders (EDI and EOD ordering) and corresponding invoices. Library vendors should support a number of ILS systems for approval or slip ordering. Major library vendors also offer shelf-ready options for approval or slip order books, which can effectively save staff time (especially in larger libraries). Shelf-ready books may arrive with a call number, barcode, an enhanced library binding, or other library customization. Shelf-ready titles, however, typically would not be subject to return.[14] New acquisitions librarians setting up an approval or slip plan (or changing aspects of an existing approval plan) will need to work with the cataloging and other departments to design the appropriate acquisitions workflow.

Standing Orders

Standing orders are defined as non-periodical serials or continuations, as opposed to journals, with an ongoing contractual obligation between the library and the vendor to purchase each volume published until completion of the series or cancellation by the publisher or library. Standing orders can be in print or electronic formats, and while materials placed on standing order vary from library to library, they typically include both monographic and continuing resources. Examples include annuals, yearbooks, almanacs, multivolume sets, conference proceedings, numbered and unnumbered monographic series with individual titles, non-monographic serials with volume numbers, and supplements.

The advantage of placing materials on standing order over individual firm orders is the assurance that every volume published in the series is automatically received. However, as they are a contractual expense, the acquisitions librarian needs to ensure the allocation of funds for their continuing cost. In addition, some safeguard should be in place to prevent individual firm orders for a title that is already on standing order. Standing orders may be both regularly and irregularly published with the result that the cost and number of volumes printed vary from year to year. These variances make it difficult for the acquisitions librarian to project costs or to receive price quotes. When establishing a new standing order, it is helpful to inquire from the publisher how many volumes are expected in the series as well as the projected publishing schedule. It is also good to remember that while these materials were once considered essential to the collection, they may not necessarily be so today. All continuations require periodic review for quality, scope, and relevance to the collection.

Standing orders can be placed with vendors, such as GOBI Library Solutions, ProQuest, or directly from a publisher. The decision to place a standing order directly with the publisher or through a book vendor depends on each library's ordering practices as well as the publisher terms. Some publishers, including many smaller presses, require orders placed directly through them, while others do not accept standing orders and require ordering through a vendor. Whichever service an acquisitions librarian chooses, the goal of acquiring materials in a timely manner should be a high priority. There are many advantages to ordering continuations as standing orders from a book vendor, but the primary benefits are the discounts offered for agreeing to purchase all volumes, and the ease of ordering and making claims. Quality control is an additional service that larger, established book vendors, such as GOBI Library Solutions, are able to offer libraries. They typically receive the items from the publishers before sending them on to the library with the invoice. By offering quality control before shipping to a library, they ensure that libraries do not receive defective or duplicate items.

NOTES

1. William H. Walters, "Patron-Driven Acquisition and the Educational Mission of the Academic Library," *Library Resources & Technical Services* 56, no. 3 (2012): 199. doi:10.5860/lrts.56n3.
2. Aaron Wood, "Mainstream Patron-Driven Acquisition: Topicality Over the Scholarly Record ... and the Cello Suites," *Against the Grain* 25, no. 5 (2013): 22.
3. National Information Standards Organization (NISO), *Demand Driven Acquisition of Monographs: A Recommended Practice of the National Information Standards Organization* (Baltimore: National Information Standards Organization, 2014), accessed June 1, 2019, https://groups.niso.org/apps/group_public/download.php/13373/rp-20-2014_DDA.pdf.
4. Robert F. Nardini, "Approval Plans," in Encyclopedia of Library and Information Science, ed. Miriam A. Drake (New York [etc.]: Mercel Dekker, 2003), 133. doi: 10.1081/E-ELIS 120008874
5. Ibid.
6. Jesse Holden, *Acquisitions: Core Concepts and Practices* (Chicago: ALA Neal-Schuman, 2017), 43.
7. Ibid.
8. Robert F. Nardini, "Approval Plans," in Encyclopedia of Library and Information Science, ed. Miriam A. Drake (New York [etc.]: Mercel Dekker, 2003), 135. doi: 10.1081/E-ELIS 120008874

9. Carmelita Pickett and Simona Tabacaru and Jeanne Harrell. "E-Approval Plans in Research Libraries," *College & Research Libraries* 75, no. 2 (March 2014): 226. doi: 10.5860/crl12-410

10. Stephen Bosch et al., "Do Libraries Still Need Book Vendors and Subscription Agents?" *z687: Creating the Future of Technical Services*, October 2011, 1–2. doi: 10339/36393

11. Robert F. Nardini, "Approval Plans," in Encyclopedia of Library and Information Science, ed. Miriam A. Drake (New York [etc.]: Mercel Dekker, 2003), 134. doi: 10.1081/E-ELIS 120008874

12. Ibid.

13. Ibid.

14. Ibid. 135

CHAPTER **THREE**

Things You Might Encounter

The bulk of acquisitions will involve managing a budget and ordering materials. There are also additional tasks that an acquisitions librarian may be asked to complete. Chapter 4 provides an overview of additional tasks you may be asked to take on or perform, giving you a basic knowledge of what each responsibility may entail. This is not an exhaustive list by any means and reflects some of the evolving demands placed on acquisitions librarians.

FORECASTING

Every library has a strategic plan that reflects the mission, values, and both short-term and long-term goals for the library. The acquisitions librarian understands that budgeting is an important part of collection development and a management tool for fulfilling a library's mission to its community; it is a financial statement of the library's vision and helps determine the services and resources offered. The budget development process is ongoing throughout the year, and the acquisitions librarian uses forecasting to predict the use of the current budget as well as to predict future fiscal year budgets. Materials budgets are created annually based on existing criteria for current resources, while forecasting provides an informed guess as to what these resources will cost in the coming fiscal year. Long-term planning, three to five years in advance, absolutely requires budget forecasting to form the blueprint that turns dreams into reality. Without forecasting, effective planning for new resources cannot take place. Directors, administrators, and library boards require periodic budget status reports and strategic budgeting using forecasting methods gives the acquisitions librarian the ability to provide reports quickly and accurately.

There are multiple methods of developing a spending forecast and the type used will depend on the budgeting method and organizational requirements. Spreadsheet software, like Excel, offers the acquisitions librarian a tool to develop a forecast for the materials budget. A typical forecast will span three years from the current fiscal year. On the spreadsheet, enter expenditures with as much information as possible, including renewal period, the number of volumes received, total invoiced amount, PO number, budgeted amount, estimated remaining budget, and the actual amount paid. Pay close attention to the budgeted amount and the actual amount paid. One method of forecasting, which works well with zero-based budgeting, involves analyzing previous inflation rates to project future inflation rates. Use the formula (new value-original value)/original value to analyze the percentage of change for each resource across the fiscal year to determine the increase pattern. For example, if a standing order cost $200 in 2018 and $215.00 in 2019, the formula = (215-200)/200 demonstrates there was an eight percent increase. Now that you know the rate of increase, multiply the current year pricing by the rate of increase to give the price forecast for the next fiscal year. A more general but less precise method, which works with incremental line-item budgeting, is to multiply each line item by the same average percent. Not planning for expected increases, yields a materials budget that does not adequately represent the resources needed to pay for all expenditures.

BUDGET REDUCTIONS AND CANCELLATIONS

An academic library funding model is set by the campus administration, while a public library receives their funding from state and local sources. The amount of funding is what determines the resources a library offers, as well as serving as an influence on the quality of its services. However, economic events, such as low enrollment or decreased funding availability will almost certainly require trimming the materials budget. This unfortunate reality means there will come a time when the administration requests the acquisitions librarian to cut the materials budget significantly, sometimes even in the middle of a current fiscal year. What is the best approach to balancing decreased funding allocations while maintaining quality service?

First, to help abate any budget crisis rumors on campus or with the public, remain calm and keep any initial budget discussions within the library and with only those qualified to discuss budgetary decisions. Remember that budgeting is an ongoing assessment tool, and part of the duties for an acquisitions librarian is to be knowledgeable about all aspects of the materials budget, including currently committed funds and projected funding needs in coming fiscal years. Resources and service costs increase every year, and the acquisitions librarian should always be prepared to identify areas of the materials budget where cuts can take place. Knowledge of the library's strategic plan and the ability to forecast budget requirements will assist the acquisitions librarian in ensuring the financial solvency of the library while maintaining services.

Approval plans, blanket orders, and firm orders are the first places to look to trim the budget immediately. However, cutting the budget for approvals, blanket or firm orders, is only a stopgap measure at best, as you cannot expect the same level of immediate budget reduction success without large-scale cancellations in additional categories. When evaluating where the cuts should occur, remember that databases, journals, and standing orders are contractual obligations and cannot be reduced or eliminated without checking the license agreement for cancellation penalties or required notification of intent to cancel. Contractual commitments, such as databases and standing orders, have varying renewal dates and the acquisitions librarian should know these as well as allowable time frames for cancellation. Knowing the renewal dates is crucial to avoid renewing an unwanted resource. Annually reviewing continuing resources often yields potential cancellations where funds can be redirected. The criteria used to evaluate continuing resources should include cost per use; format if electronic is preferred; duplication in coverage with existing resources; and whether or not a resource is still needed. It may also be helpful to review other resources that may provide similar content for a lower cost or package deals that may increase access to content for a reduced price. Remember, library materials not used or accessed are a poor return on investment, and it is important to have facts and usage statistics to back up any proposed cancellation.

Other resources, such as standing orders, journal packages, and approval plans may require additional consideration. Standing orders involve a commitment to purchase all the issued volumes in a series and may be both active and inactive in their publication status. A full review of all the standing orders, not just those received regularly, may provide the opportunity to cancel those no longer necessary, completed, or discontinued. The first step is to run an open standing order report. Next, email publishers or research publisher and vendor websites, as well as online Ulrich serials database, to identify completed series, discontinued series, or otherwise permanently inactive. Information on future volumes is typically available on the vendor website or the individual publisher's website. Finally, analyze usage statistics to identify those not accessed and then coordinate with collection development to decide whether to continue or discontinue the standing order. It is important that the acquisitions librarian, in concert with the collection development librarian, assess not only the usage of all standing orders but also how the standing order titles meet collection needs before considering cancellation. With this information in hand, check with the vendor on the cancellation period. While it is true that due to publishing timeframes some series titles cannot be canceled before receipt, future volumes could be canceled thus freeing funds for upcoming fiscal years.

Journal packages allow libraries access to journals and journal archives for the length of the subscription term. Publishers and vendors offer a large collection at a discounted price over purchasing a subscription to individual titles. Similar to databases, they are contractual obligations that are renewed annually and cannot be canceled midstream. However, continue to evaluate them for future budget reductions. As journal packages generally include many titles, the question to ask is how useful the overall package is to the collection, library, or users. Research those with overlap within other databases for ease of use, breadth, and unique content. Consider eliminating subscriptions where information is duplicated or available elsewhere.

Approval plans, blanket orders, and firm orders are typically not contractual obligations making these line items the primary areas to look at for budget cuts. The first step is to cancel any general blanket or approval plans that are automatically processed and shipped. The library may wish to pause or stop an approval plan, rather than cancel it entirely. The approval plan can then be resumed when more money becomes available—even several years later. Next, any plans tied to demand-driven programs should have the purchase parameters reset plus the amount allocated for purchases reduced, redistributed, or canceled. Finally, all firm order purchasing should cease unless necessary for current course work or programs.

REPORTS

All acquisition librarians must plan to create accurate and timely annual budget reports in addition to smaller periodic updates on the budget status. Budget reports compare the budget with actual results and serve as a blueprint for the financial health of the organization, as well as an economic planning tool. Any deviation or variances, from the original budget, must be explained in detail. Public institutions make all budgets and financial reports available to the public for review on either their library web page or as part of the governing organization web page. Academic libraries typically prepare an annual budget report. ILS reports can generate total expenditures by format.

The characteristics that make an excellent budget report are:

> **Clarity.** It should be readily understood by the library director, budget administrator, finance director, board member, and any city governing boards.

Accuracy. It should be an accurate and precise representation of the budget with valid budget figures, backed up with hard data.

Consistency. As budgets are economic comparison tools, it should be constructed consistently to allow comparisons between budgeting periods and fiscal years.

Concise yet comprehensive. It should include as much information as possible to ensure a complete understanding of the budget but should also be concise. Be sure to include both revenue and expenditures, but do not include extraneous information such as inferences or conjecture.

There are many kinds of reports that can be generated from an ILS that are useful to an acquisitions librarian. Reports can be used for analysis, to provide information, or to initiate action.

Some examples of useful reports are:

Open orders: Once a month, a report is run showing all the purchase orders that are open. This means that the item has not been received. Location such as library stacks, approval, graphic novels, or vendor can be used to sort the report. Open orders that are older than three months, for example, are then investigated. The acquisitions librarian can create a spreadsheet with orders to investigate and give to the appropriate person to follow up. By checking on open orders once a month, it makes it easier at the end of the year to make sure all items are paid and received.

Collection development monthly budget report: This is a snapshot of the ledger for a given month. It is broken out by parent fund (Approvals, Serials, Collection Maintenance). It also calculates the percentage of remaining funds available.

Serials review: This is a suite of queries used to compile financial data on serials expenditures across a defined period and can be helpful in evaluating electronic resources.

Receiving reports: A report can be generated to identify those eBook orders that have requestors associated with the order. The report can show open eBook orders that have the notes field populated with hold/notify contact information.

Lost books: Helpful to get a list of titles that are marked "lost" to project how much will be spent in the new fiscal year to replace them.

Bib records with no items: It is helpful to get a list of titles that have a bibliographic record but do not have an item attached. The process of figuring out where the material is should start in acquisitions.

Outstanding claims: For use with the claiming option for continuations.

Reports that compare last year's invoices to this year's expected invoices: As the fiscal year is ending, it is good to know what invoices are expected.

VENDOR NEGOTIATION

When you request a price quote for a new resource, either as a direct purchase or a subscription, it is important to understand that pricing is negotiable. You can and should request lower pricing or other pricing options. Many publishers and vendors are willing to negotiate pricing if it means acquiring you as a customer. In cases where a publisher or vendor will not budge on price, you can explore other options such as similar products offered through other providers or investigate consortia pricing. Publishers and vendors who operate on a calendar year may also be very open to negotiating subscription costs in mid-November through the end of December. Negotiation should also happen during renewal. When you see an eight percent price increase on an invoice, phone the rep and ask for justification for the increase. While asking about a price increase may not always result in a cost reduction, it is possible that the vendor will offer additional content or other pricing options to keep you as a customer. If nothing else, you have registered your concern over the large price increase, and this may result in the vendor or publisher not increasing prices so much in the following year. One of the key elements in any negotiation process is to put forth your request, and then stop talking. Listen to the vendor and let them fill the uncomfortable silence.

You may also negotiate the terms and wording of a license agreement. In some cases, you may want to request wording that would allow the library to terminate the subscription if the budget situation suddenly changes. You always have the option to walk away from a negotiation or request to cancel a subscription. In some cases, canceling a needed resource is a very difficult decision and may not always be possible.

ASSESSMENT

The general definition of assessment in a library is to measure user needs and determine how well the library is meeting those needs through its services and resources. Assessment may be driven by upper management or may come from within a unit wanting to evaluate how work is done. In thinking about assessment in acquisitions, identify what questions should be addressed, and what data will be needed to complete the assessment.

For assessment, the acquisitions librarian should become familiar with data sources, and who is responsible for collecting the data. It may also be helpful to have conversations with other units in the library to find out what data or statistics they may need.

Assessment projects in acquisitions may involve analyzing expenditures, allocation formulas, circulation of new acquisitions to determine if collecting efforts and budgets should change, interlibrary loan data, circulation data, or cost-per-use.

Database subscriptions should be reviewed annually prior to renewal. The review process starts with gathering cost data. The acquisitions librarian may either generate a report from the ILS that pulls cost data from invoices or use Excel to track this data. To get a more precise cost, analyze three years of cost data consisting of the current year's cost plus the previous two years' worth of cost. Next, pull the usage statistics for every database. In academic libraries, statistics data may be acquired through a paid service service such as ProQuest with downloadable COUNTER reports. However, as there are vendors who are not COUNTER compliant, not all the usage data is captured. If this is the case, the vendors must be contacted directly for their usage statistics. When assessing individual titles, some of the factors that librarians consider are:

Cost-per-use. If cost-per-use is very high, then the librarian might consider other factors to make a cancellation decision such as continued need for the resource.

Is there a program in the subject area, or at least a class that covers the topic? Even if there isn't a program, the sort of research indexed by a database may prove useful. For example, Medline may be important to support programs in psychology or public health even if the school does not have a medical program.

Are there other databases in the same subject area? It may be preferable to keep multiple databases in that subject. (For example, PsycInfo and ProQuest Psychology Journals index sophisticated research, but may also be useful to a more general population of undergraduates or non-majors).

Assessment in acquisitions may also involve assessing workflows, processes, or position descriptions with the goal towards improvement, increased efficiencies, and alignment of staff responsibilities with current needs.

MONOGRAPH SUBSCRIPTIONS

Libraries have other options for acquiring monographs aside from firm order purchases and approval plans. Many vendors offer eBook subscription packages that provide selected eBook titles for a yearly fee. Some of these products also include magazines, newspapers, film, and audio. While establishing a single purchase order for the subscription is straightforward, acquisitions may need to work closely with catalogers to ensure the download of vendor records to make the items discoverable. In addition to eBook subscriptions, some vendors offer a subscription service for print monographs. For example, the Junior Library Guild (JLG) offers a subscription service for children and juvenile materials. JLG is similar to an approval plan where categories are selected and then materials are shipped monthly based on the categories selected. It differs from an approval plan in that the number of categories selected determines the subscription cost. Another monograph subscription service is the Brodart McNaughton collection, which offers varied pricing models. Libraries can select the pricing model that best fits their budget and needs and then select popular titles to ship monthly. Using subscription monograph services will most likely involve cataloging staff to ensure item records are available for discovery.

STREAMING MEDIA ACQUISITIONS

The current demand for streamed media content appears to be surpassing the demand for other content in libraries and continues to be in a state of flux. Currently, there exist a substantial number of streamed media content providers working with both academic and public libraries. Most streaming media providers include public performance rights in films offered and provide access to their content through course management systems like Canvas, Moodle, or Blackboard. A few providers such as *Overdrive* and *Hoopla* provide streamed media content as well as eBook and audio content. *Kanopy* offers a DDA program for media which requires close monitoring of usage so expenditures do not get out of control. Librarians new to acquisitions should be aware of the types of streaming video content available to libraries along with evolving issues with streamed media providers.

Librarians responsible for acquiring streaming content should consider a number of factors before making a purchase such as cost, pricing models, hosting fees, available discounts, and usage restrictions. In some instances, if a faculty member requests a film that is only available through one provider, inquire if an a la carte lease is possible versus a subscription to the entire database. Acquisitions librarians should check with their consortia for discounted pricing. It may also be a possibility to arrange a mini consortia for a streaming collection if other libraries are interested in a subscription or purchase. A vendor is usually willing to adjust pricing if several libraries are interested in acquiring their resources. If considering a collection, a trial is always desirable in order to evaluate the content of a streaming collection. Technical considerations should also be evaluated, including streaming quality, HD availability, captioning, sound quality, and if any technical adjustments to local network infrastructure (or from the vendor) will be required. Streaming quality on mobile devices should also be evaluated. Whether a single title or a large subscription, librarians should ask vendors about MARC availability. MARC records provide an important access point for patrons using a catalog or discovery system, and ideally, the records should be available and included in the subscription or purchase price.

Streaming video platforms often offer a number of useful features designed to manage content for optimal viewing. Many streaming platforms allow users to create an account, which may be required to use some of these advanced features such as customizing video segments. Customization can be particularly useful for faculty who only wish to share certain parts of a video to their students or for students needing only a segment of a film in a presentation. As with other electronic databases, a citation feature is available with most streaming media providers. Of course features will vary on platforms from vendor to vendor, but many of these options (for example, creating playlists or embedding videos in a course management system) should be the standard on most streaming platforms.

Marketing streaming collections to students, faculty, or public library patrons is an important consideration. Acquisitions librarians should work with the appropriate library departments to ensure that streaming video collections are effectively marketed to library patrons. Streaming video collections can easily be promoted through presentations, bibliographic instructions sessions, on social media, library image galleries, and news releases.

Acquisitions librarians may be asked by the library administration to provide usage statistics for the annual ACRL survey, IPEDS, ARL survey, or for other annual reports (or to maintain in-house use statistics). The administrative portal for a streaming video collection should offer a number of useful reports to generate usage statistics. The latest versions of COUNTER reports (Release 5 at the time of this writing) will be available for this purpose from many vendors, and statistical surveys should designate which reports are acceptable to use. Reports are usually very easy to generate by date, with standard output options to save files in Excel, PDF, and other formats. COUNTER and other database statistics are important factors to consider when making decisions to renew or cancel streaming collections.

MARC records for all of a library's accessible streaming video titles should also be available from the administrative portal. MARC record functionality may vary slightly according to the vendor, but libraries usually have the option to download a complete base file or new records (including updated or deleted titles) on a monthly basis. Filters allow librarians to download records for specific collections, if desired. Providers may send automated messages when new titles are added or deleted (with the availability of corresponding MARC records). After any new streaming service is acquired, the librarian (or possibly staff member) responsible for managing the MARC records should be provided with credentials to access the administrative portal and set up to receive any automated MARC related notifications. The acquisitions librarian should also share the portal login credentials with other appropriate departments as needed (for example, the systems or electronic resources librarian may need access in order to configure the proxy settings).

As with any electronic resource, accessing a library's licensed content from the various streaming video providers requires some form of authentication for authorized users. Most (if not all) of the major vendors will allow users to access streaming video content both on and off campus with proper authentication. The acquisitions or systems librarian will provide the institution's campus IP range to the vendor, which will allow users on campus to view streaming content without inputting their login credentials. Authorized users from off campus, however, will need to authenticate with their individualized login credentials—usually a username and password—which serves to identify authorized users (faculty or students enrolled at the university or college or library card information for public library patrons) for remote access. Proxy software, for example OCLC's EZproxy, can be used to add a proxy prefix to the database web address which allows only authorized users affiliated with the institution to access the content. Streaming video providers should support commonly used authentication software or services, like Shibboleth, Single Sign On, or may even allow users to log in with an account name and password (or to possibly sign in using Facebook). An acquisitions librarian may need to work with the electronic resources or systems librarian to enable user authentication. Technical support to resolve authentication issues is usually provided by the vendor.

CHAPTER **FOUR**

Tools of the Trade

There are aspects of acquisitions work that are considered basic "tools of the trade" that you will want to become familiar with. Keep in mind that acquisitions work varies from one library to the next so some of the tools listed may not be widely applicable.

PURCHASING CARD

Many libraries will allow library staff or departments to have purchasing cards or pCards. Having a purchasing card makes it much easier to order material from vendors who only take credit cards and provides flexibility in obtaining rush items or items that are out of print. The acquisitions librarian should be familiar with the institutional policies that govern the use of the purchasing card and should know the people in the accounts payable and procurement offices.

RECONCILIATION

As already noted, many libraries use a different financial system that is separate from the larger organization. In cases of a separate accounts payable department, it may be necessary for the acquisitions staff to ensure invoices are paid. Therefore, it is key to have a good working relationship with the accounts payable department. Reports can be run to show what invoices have been paid and questions can be directed to the accounts payable liaison.

NAVIGATING THE BUILDING BLOCKS OF THE ACQUISITIONS MODULE OF YOUR ILS

For the librarian new to acquisitions, much of the daily work will involve navigating and using the acquisitions module of their library's ILS (integrated library system). Academic libraries use a variety of integrated library systems supported by various vendors, but each ILS (regardless of vendor) will have modules specific to technical services with modules dedicated to cataloging, serials, and acquisitions. It is important for a new librarian to understand the overall purpose and basic functions of the acquisitions module and learn to use modules efficiently. The module is used for a variety of essential tasks, including creating purchase orders, invoicing, receiving items, managing funds, and submitting orders to vendors. The ILS is also used for running a variety of acquisitions reports (covered in Chapter 3). The acquisitions module can seem somewhat technical and daunting at first, but developing an understanding of these basic functions will greatly help new acquisitions librarians to perform their work competently.

A librarian suddenly new to acquisitions will undoubtedly have many questions about the basic workflow used in their ILS module. For example, how does a book order get placed? Why is an order assigned to a particular vendor or encumbered to a specific fund code? How is an invoice created and paid, and how does it link to a certain order? What if a mistake is made—can an order or invoice be modified? How does the ILS help to balance the budget and track subject liaison spending? What are some of the common ILS reports used in acquisitions work? The ILS acquisitions module is designed to facilitate acquisitions work with these types of questions in mind, and to help librarians and staff successfully carry out the essential work of acquiring books and other materials. In many libraries, an acquisitions librarian may supervise staff charged with creating orders while in other libraries, the acquisitions librarian will be placing the order directly so in either case, a good working knowledge of ordering is essential.

The vendor record is an important starting point for understanding the ordering process. Librarians and acquisitions staff will usually create and place an order with a particular book or audiovisual vendor. Libraries also place orders with smaller vendors that may specialize in certain types of book sales like nursing, musical scores, film producers, and streaming video. A library may also place orders with a particular press, like a university press, or a vendor selling out of print or remainder books. Most libraries will regularly place orders with several vendors. A vendor record is created in the ILS containing information about the specific vendor and may include vendor addresses and contact information, discount, performance, customer number, and notes about the vendor. A vendor record functions as the central point of reference for placing an order and is linked to the purchase order and subsequent invoice. Most vendor records will probably already appear in the ILS, but if an order is placed with a new vendor, the acquisitions librarian (or staff) can easily create a new vendor record. It may be helpful for a librarian new to acquisitions to review some of the vendor records used in recent ordering cycles to become familiar with the vendors used in the ordering process. The vendor record should display a list of orders placed in a given ordering cycle.

The ILS is used to create a purchase order for books and other materials ordered from a vendor. The technical process and nuances may vary depending on the library and ILS, but in general, a basic order is created by selecting a vendor record, an order type, and a fund code (or fund ID) for each title ordered. For example, a firm purchase order for a book is created by selecting the appropriate vendor and charging (or encumbering) the title to a fund code (or fund ID) assigned to a certain subject discipline. If a large number of books are ordered, an order line for each book listing the title, the price, and the fund code (and possibly other information) would appear in the purchase order. A MARC record for each title ordered is downloaded into the ILS from OCLC or other bibliographic utility prior to creating the purchase order (or as part of the automated ordering process). Depending on the workflow, a library may create a single purchase order listing a large number of books, or simply a purchase order with one or two items. A purchase order could also include a note to notify a faculty member when the title arrives, the name of the librarian selecting the title, or additional budget details. The ILS will automatically assign a number to each purchase order created in the acquisitions department.

The ILS purchase order is an exact record of the books and other materials placed in each order to a vendor, and the amount spent on the order. For example, if a library places an online order with a vendor using an order cart, a purchase order will need to be created in the ILS (using the vendor record) listing the books and the amount spent on the order. The ILS purchase order should exactly correspond to the actual order placed online for accurate accounting. The purchase order can be displayed at any time in the ILS module and will include the title of the item, total amount spent, the amount spent for each item, funded (or encumbered) amounts, the date the order was created, and whether or not an item has been received or invoiced. The purchase order is essential for tracking library materials ordered and acquisitions spending during the fiscal year.

An invoice is usually created in the ILS for each electronic or paper invoice received from the vendor. The ILS invoice will match the electronic or paper invoice (and invoice number), with an invoice line created for each listed item with the amount invoiced. The invoice links, line by line, to the ILS purchase order, moving the encumbered amount on the purchase order to an invoiced status in the ILS ledger. In some cases, the amount on the invoice will differ from the purchase order amount due to discounts applied at the time of invoicing. It is important to note that a single purchase order may have order lines linked to more than one invoice, and an invoice may contain item lines linked to one or more ILS purchase orders. Some books or materials placed in an order may be out of stock or shipped separately, and these items then appear on subsequent invoices either separately or with books listed on other ILS purchase orders. Methods for creating invoices will vary depending on the

ILS, but the process should include a few easy steps for each line. The invoice may also need to be modified and saved, depending on the workflow in place at the library. An ILS invoice will likely contain several elements, including the vendor, the invoice number, the purchase order number, the titles, the fiscal cycle, paid status, amounts, and date created. The ILS should have an option to display each line in detail, and offer other useful functions, like linking to the purchase order or displaying the order line. The invoicing ILS component should be fairly easy to learn and to navigate and serves as an essential component of the acquisitions module.

The ILS acquisitions module functions as an accounting system to accurately reflect invoice payments made directly to the vendors. The acquisitions librarian or staff may use a purchase card to pay a vendor when the order is placed or pay when an invoice arrives. The library's acquisitions department may pay these vendor invoices or may send the invoices to a library accounting department or university or college purchasing office (or possibly a combination of these methods, depending on the library). Regardless of the method of payment, the acquisitions department will subsequently pay the corresponding invoices in the ILS to reflect the actual payments made to the vendors. The invoice created in the ILS is retrieved by the invoice number, checked for accuracy against the electronic or paper invoice, and then paid (using a pay invoice function). Once an invoice is paid, the payment status in the ILS changes the amount from the invoiced column to the paid column in the accounting ledger. The best practice, depending on the workflow of the acquisitions department, is to pay invoices in the ILS on a regular weekly or monthly basis. The original invoices received from the vendors are also usually kept and printed (if electronic) and filed in paper format, or saved electronically. A university or college may have an institutional policy regarding the number of years to retain paper files.

In some cases, purchase orders and invoices require modification. For example, a purchase order may need cancellation if the incorrect book (or item in another format) is ordered, or if an item remains out of stock for the remainder of the fiscal year (if these items are not rolled over to the next fiscal year). Or perhaps an incorrect or incomplete MARC record gets downloaded for an order, requiring a modification in the purchase order line. An invoice could also require modification reflecting a credit refund, or an error might occur with the wrong amount invoiced by the vendor (or by acquisitions department). Sometimes a technical error can occur with the ILS, or more likely a human error, perhaps related to prorating shipping amounts or other error during the ordering or invoicing process. Fortunately, an ILS acquisitions module will include functions to modify purchase orders or invoices. For example, an order line can be easily modified to change a holding code or to charge the book to a different fund ID. The ILS should also include some options for changing the amount of the order, or perhaps cancelling a title, or deleting the entire purchase order. Likewise, an ILS should have options to reverse a payment or to modify an invoice line by changing the amount. Invoices can also be deleted, locked and unlocked, or linked to a different order or fiscal cycle. Additional lines can always be added to both purchase orders and invoices or adjusted according to the circumstances.

The ILS acquisitions module is also used to receive books and other library materials. The receive orders function can retrieve the title of the book, DVD, or other items listed on the purchase order. Received items are checked against a packing slip and marked received in the ILS. Receiving the books in the ILS allows the acquisitions department to run reports on items paid for but not received, and to place claims on these orders not received from the vendor. Receiving orders functions as both a tracking and auditing tool and serves as proof that a library has received all items ordered and purchased. Receiving books in the ILS is a relatively simple process, compared to creating more complex purchase orders or invoices. In some libraries, student workers manually unpack book shipments and receive the books in the ILS.

Many libraries take advantage of EDI (Electronic Data Interchange) or EOD (Embedded Order Data) to order most of their books from vendors without having to manually build purchase orders and invoices. Most of the major library book vendors support EDI or EOD ordering and automated invoicing. Libraries use file formats (9XX or X12, for example) in their ILS reports to automatically create purchase orders and corresponding invoices.

EDI or EOD orders are placed in an online bibliographic database, such as GOBI Library Solutions or OASIS, and the vendor provides a batch of matching MARC records for the library to import into the ILS. It offers great time savings especially for libraries ordering large numbers of books. Instead of spending time searching and downloading individual MARC records and keying in purchase order information for each book line by line, libraries can submit batch orders simply by running a series of reports in the ILS. The ILS automatically creates purchase orders and running another series of reports creates the corresponding invoices from a file sent by the vendor. Setting up EDI or EOD ordering in the ILS can be a very technical process and may require assistance from the library services and ILS vendors (or an in-house systems librarian). However, once automated ordering is set up, running the reports is smooth and efficient, though troubleshooting can sometimes require library systems expertise. Most libraries will not exclusively use EDI or EOD ordering, so it is still important for a new acquisitions librarian to learn to create purchase orders and invoices for ordering from other vendors.

HELP USING THE ILS ACQUISITIONS MODULE

The best way to learn the acquisitions module is to train with a staff member already familiar with the system. It may not be necessary for the acquisitions librarian to use every feature of the module, but it is important to have an overall familiarity with the system. Often there is a point person in the library or within a group of libraries who interacts with the ILS provider and can be contacted for help. Subscribing to ILS listservs is also an important tool to learning and staying familiar with any ILS. The ILS should also have a help section within the system and the ILS provider may have a website that provides training material. There may also be a user group for the ILS and an option to visit local libraries using the same ILS for additional training and support.

EXCEL

Excel is a much-used tool in acquisitions work for a variety of important tasks. Many reports run in a library's ILS usually are configured to open in Excel. For example, expenditure reports are necessary to view in Excel (where sums can be calculated and data sorted by order type) and bibliographic lists of purchases run by subject or fund code which may be used for accreditation or other purposes. Vendors will often provide lists of titles in Excel, which are useful to sort by publication date, publisher, or other criteria helpful for evaluating an electronic product. Becoming familiar with Excel, the types of filters available in Excel, and the basic and more advanced equations will help librarians with many functions of acquisitions.

CURRENT MONOGRAPH VENDORS

Monograph vendors will often reach out to acquisitions personnel to obtain the libraries business. If you are taking on acquisitions responsibilities, your library may already have an established monograph vendor. If you are contacted by a monograph vendor or tasked with investigating or establishing a new monograph vendor, this section provides a briefly annotated list of current monograph vendors to help you gain some familiarity with the market.

AbeBooks
Like Alibris, AbeBooks primarily sells older books but also offers options to purchase current titles through third-party sellers. *www.abebooks.com*

Alibris for Libraries
Primarily a source for out-of-print titles and older in-print titles, but also newer titles. Accepts purchase orders. *http://library.alibris.com/about-library*

Amazon
Provides purchase option for current and older monographs and videos. Requires purchase card or establishment of corporate account to facilitate heavy volume of ordering. *www.amazon.com*

Baker and Taylor
Leading distributor of books, video, and music products to public and school libraries. Accepts purchase orders. *www.btol.com/library.cfm*

Better World Books
Seeks donations of books to sell online. Like Alibris and AbeBooks, BWB primarily sells older materials but may also have more current and popular titles available. *www.betterworldbooks.com/*

Book Depository
Based in Great Britain, they have more than 17 million titles and offer free delivery worldwide. Good source for European publications. Credit cards only. *https://www.bookdepository.com/*

Daedalus
Specializes in selling remainder books and overstock music CDs and videos. *www.daedalusbooks.com/*

GOBI Library Solutions from EBSCO
(Formerly YBP Library Services) GOBI Library Solutions Provides acquisition, collection development, and technical services to academic and research libraries around the world. Accepts purchase orders. *www.ebsco.com/products/gobi-library-solutions*

EBSCOhost Collection Manager
Source for eBooks and audiobooks. Ordering available by individual title, collections, or PDA. *www.ebsco.com/products/ebooks*

Emery Pratt
Provides firm orders, cataloging/processing, collection development, continuations and standing orders, and out-of-print search service for libraries. Accepts purchase orders. *https://emery-pratt.com/*

Harrassowitz
German academic publishing house that provides acquisitions, standing orders, databases, and collection development services to academic and research libraries. Excellent source to track down esoteric European publications. Accepts purchase orders. *www.harrassowitz.de/*

Ingram Content Group
Offers one of the largest selections of books and audiobooks with a large inventory for public, school, and academic libraries. Additional services offered include standing order and continuations, print-on-demand titles, and shelf-ready cataloging and processing options. Accepts purchase orders. *www.ingramcontent.com*

Marcial Pons
Spanish-based Company specializing in tracking down publications from Spanish speaking countries. Accepts purchase orders. *www.marcialpons.es/*

Midwest Library Service
Provides firm orders, cataloging/processing, collection development, continuations and standing orders, and out-of-print search service for libraries. Accepts purchase orders. *www.midwestls.com/*

ProQuest OASIS
A web-based system for searching, selecting, and ordering print and electronic books for academic, corporate, and government libraries. Accepts purchase orders. *www.proquest.com/products-services/OASIS.html*

Rittenhouse R2 Digital Library
An eBook platform for health science collections featuring a comprehensive collection of medical, nursing, and allied health eBooks. *www.rittenhouse.com/Rbd/web/ContentPage.aspx?Config=R2Library*

CURRENT STANDING ORDER VENDORS

Baker and Taylor
Offers series standing orders to public and school libraries. They have a web-based system and offer free management reports. Continuations offerings include numbered and unnumbered monographic series, sets in progress, non-subscription serials, proceedings, and select U.S. government documents and publications. *www.baker-taylor.com/ps_details.cfm?id=39*

GOBI Library Solutions
Formerly YBP Library Services, they offer series standing orders to public, school, academic, and research libraries. They receive the materials from the publisher and then send them to the library. Provides a web-based system with advanced search and filtering for ease of ordering,

reporting features, and detailed bibliographic records. Also, provides notification of publishing delays or cancellations. Can cancel at any time, however, if a volume is on its way then the cancellation will not go into effect until after that volume has been supplied to the library.
https://gobi.ebsco.com/gobi

Harrassowitz
German-based publishing house provides print and electronic standing orders service for monographic series, irregular series, sets in progress, proceedings, annuals, loose-leaf publications, and yearbooks. Specializing in publications from Europe, Russia, Egypt, Israel, India, Sri Lanka, Japan, Australia, New Zealand, and South Africa. Can cancel at any time, however, if a volume has shipped then the cancellation will not go into effect until after that volume has been supplied to the library.
www.harrassowitz.de/standing-orders.html

Ingram Content Services
Offers a wide range of standing order programs for public, school, and academic libraries with a choice between automatic shipment and notification only.
www.ingramcontent.com

Midwest Library Services
Offers series print standing orders for academic and public libraries from U.S. publishers only. Categories include monographic and non-monographic, numbered and unnumbered, regular and irregular, proceedings, yearbooks, and annuals. They do not provide magazines, journals, or loose-leaf updating services. Discounts range from list price to 10 percent. *www.midwestls.com/Home*

ProQuest OASIS
A web-based system for searching, selecting, and ordering print, standing orders and electronic books for academic, corporate, and government libraries. Accepts purchase orders. *www.proquest.com/products-services/OASIS.html*

COMMON PUBLISHERS AND VENDORS

- ProQuest
- GOBI Library Solutions from EBSCO
- Baker and Taylor
- Harrassowitz
- SAGE
- Cambridge
- Elsevier
- Springer
- Wiley
- Taylor & Francis
- Oxford
- LYRASIS
- JSTOR
- Project Muse
- Marcial Pons (Spanish materials)
- OCLC

CHAPTER **FIVE**

Relevant Resources

PROFESSIONAL DEVELOPMENT AND CONTINUING EDUCATION

Library professionals new to acquisitions work may understandably feel overwhelmed as they begin their new position. Learning the ILS acquisitions module, budgeting, college or university financial policies, the nuances of ordering and processing books and invoices, negotiating with vendors (and possibly working with licenses), acquiring and managing electronic collections, and other new tasks and responsibilities can at first seem complicated. Fortunately, acquisitions librarians have numerous opportunities to take advantage of excellent resources to facilitate their professional development and continuing education. With some effort and initiative, librarians new to the field can easily gain valuable experience and knowledge simply be exploring these resources and participating in professional activities. New acquisitions librarians can attend professional conferences, join relevant associations and committees, pursue publishing opportunities, participate in webinars and online courses, and find many other creative and rewarding ways to network and learn from their colleagues. Librarians new to acquisitions should join relevant listservs, which often provide opportunities for discussions, problem solving, and professional participation.

The American Library Association (ALA) offers extensive opportunities for professional development. Within ALA, CORE: Leadership, Infrastructure, Futures, is the most appropriate division for new acquisitions professionals to join and offers six sections and interest groups that provide opportunities to serve on relevant committees, network with other acquisitions librarians, and develop professionally. CORE sections, committees, and interest groups allow librarians to learn new professional skills and to stay current regarding important trends and issues germane to acquisitions work. Although some committees may be full (or committee appointments may be selective), librarians new to acquisitions can complete a volunteer form located on the CORE website for appointment to a committee.

In addition to opportunities to participate professionally, CORE offers online resources, fundamental courses, and Webinars, to enhance professional development. The *Fundamentals of Acquisitions* course is a six-week course covering basic budgeting and financial management; acquisitions workflow, theory, and methodology; and an introduction to the collaborative skills needed to successfully negotiate and work with vendors. The course is affordable with a number of sessions offered throughout the year.

Publications emanating from CORE, ALA divisions, and many other publishers constitute excellent resources for continuing education, and reading is perhaps one of the best ways for librarians to develop professionally. CORE publications include Monographs, News, and several journals such as *Library Resources & Technical Services*, *Library Leadership & Management*, and *ITAL Information Technology and Libraries.*

While Core is the quintessential division for acquisitions librarians, opportunities for professional development may be found in other ALA divisions. For example, the Association of College & Research Libraries (ARCL) sponsors a Technical Services Interest Group and a Scholarly Communications Committee in the

Science and Technology Section. The Reference and user Services Association (RUSA) has a Collection Development and Evaluation Section (CODES) with committees for both academic and public librarians.

Acquisitions work is complex and not one-dimensional, and new librarians should consider exploring areas of librarianship related to their work. Several (if not all) ALA divisions offer continuing education opportunities related to technology and technical services, collection development, management and finance, working with electronic resources, and other areas (both general and specialized) that can complement acquisitions work. A knowledge of new trends and issues in libraries, for example, in scholarly communications, can benefit those working in the acquisitions field.

Conferences such as the annual American Library Association conference, the Charleston Conference, and the Acquisitions Institute offer excellent opportunities for professional networking and continuing education. Acquisitions librarians will encounter a veritable smorgasbord of conference presentations, sharing and discussion sessions, and programs from numerous divisions to facilitate learning, and many of the sessions will relate directly to their acquisitions work. In addition, conference exhibits provide acquisitions librarians with opportunities to discover important new electronic resources and products, and to develop new and existing relationships with vendors and publishers. The conferences offer an invaluable opportunity to meet with other acquisitions librarians, and to compare and discuss successful projects and workflow across institutions. Often, simply discovering how other institutions acquire and manage their resources can be one of the most beneficial forms of professional development. State and regional library consortia often offer a rich array of continuing education resources provided as a part of a library's membership. A local library consortium will likely employ highly knowledgeable technical consultants, with a library degree or background to conduct webinars, moderate listserv discussions, and provide authoritative technical support and advice regarding ILS issues pertaining to the acquisitions workflow. A consortium may also host an annual regional library conference for its members, which can include sessions and presentations related to acquisitions. Conference networking and sharing opportunities with other acquisitions colleagues can be of value since members of the same consortium often use the same ILS and participate in the same consortium offers.

Librarians new to acquisitions can also participate in state library associations and possibly local affiliates of ALA divisions. Many state library associations hold annual conferences, with the opportunities to attend presentations and participate in round tables and discussion groups. State library associations often sponsor interest groups or committees devoted to collection development, technical services and acquisitions, or other areas that may relate to acquisitions. Mentoring programs that match new librarians with experienced librarians offer excellent opportunities for professional development. New acquisitions librarians should not overlook resources and opportunities at the state level to enhance their professional development.

These following publications and online professional development CORE resources may be helpful to those new to acquisitions.

Core Competencies for Acquisitions Professionals. *https://alair.ala.org/handle/11213/9058,* accessed July 22, 2019.

"Fundamentals of Acquisitions," ALA.com, accessed June 27, 2019. *www.ala.org/alcts/confevents/upcoming/webcourse/foa/ol_templ.*

BOOKS

Chapman, Liz. *Managing Acquisitions in Library and Information Services,* rev. ed. London: Facet Publishing, 2008.

Evans, G. Edward. Performance Management and Appraisal: A How-To-Do-It Manual for Librarians. New York: Neal-Schuman, 2004.

Hartnett, Eric. *Guide to Streaming Video Acquisitions.* Chicago: ALA Editions, 2019.

Holden, Jesse. *Acquisitions: Core Concepts and Practices,* 2nd ed. Chicago: Neal-Schuman, 2017.

Intner, Sheila S. and Peggy Johnson. *Fundamentals of Technical Services Management.* Chicago: American Library Association, 2008.

Johnson, Peggy. *Fundamentals of Collection Development and Management,* 3rd ed. Chicago: American Library Association, 2014.

Karrass, Chester. *Negotiating Game.* New York: HarperCollins, 1992.

Matthews, Joseph R. *Strategic Planning and Management for Library Managers.* Westport, CT: Libraries Unlimited, 2005.

Sandstrom, John and Liz Miller. *Fundamentals of Technical Services.* Chicago: Neal-Schuman, 2015.

Schmidt, Krista and Tim Carstens. *The Subject Liaison's Survival Guide to Technical Services.* Chicago: American Library Association, 2017.

VanDuinkerken, Wyona, Wndi Arant Kasper, and Jeanne Harrell. *Guide to Ethics in Acquisitions.* Chicago: Associatioin for Library Collections & Technical Services. 2014.

Verminski, Alana and Kelley Marie Blanchat. *Fundamentals of Electronic Resources Management.* Chicago: Neal-Schuman, 2017.

Ward, Suzanne M. *Guide to Implementing and Managing Patron-Drive Acquisitions.* Chicago: Acquisition Section of the Association for Library Collections & Technical Services. 2012.

Wigbels Stewart, Andream et al., eds. *Staff Development: A Practical Guide.* 4th ed. Chicago: American Library Association, 2013.

Wilkinson, Frances C., Linda K. Lewis, and Rebecca L. Lubas. *The Complete Guide to Acquisitions Management. Library and Information Science Text Series.* 2nd ed. Santa Barbara: California, Libraries Unlimited, 2015.

ARTICLES

Marien, Stacey and Bob Nardini. "Let's Get Technical: Pushing the Vendor to Improve Customer Service." *Against the Grain.* December 2015–January 2016. vol. 27, no. 6.

Mays, Antje (2005) "Training New Acquisitions and Collection Development Librarians: Some Technical and Philosophical Guideposts." *Against the Grain*, vol. 17, issue 3, article 11.

Lewis, Linda K and Pistorius, Nancy (2005) "Making the Invisible Visible: What Collection Development Needs to Know About Acquisitions." *Against the Grain*, vol. 17, issue 3, article 10.

Ostergaard, Kirsten and Rossmann, Doralyn, (2017) "There's Work to be Done: Exploring Library-Vendor Relations." *Technical Services Quarterly*, 34:1, 13-33.

Sarbanes-Oxley Act 2002. https://www.govinfo.gov/content/pkg/COMPS-1883/pdf/COMPS-1883.pdf.

JOURNALS

Against the Grain
   A journal devoted to technical service and collection development topics. There are many practitioner focused articles. The journal is the publishing arm of the Charleston Conference. www.against-the-grain.com/

Journal of Electronic Resources Librarianship
(formerly known as The Acquisitions Librarian)
   A journal that focuses on all topics related to electronic resources management. www.tandfonline.com/loi/wacq20

Technical Services Quarterly
   A journal dedicated to topics concerning all aspects of technical services. www.tandfonline.com/loi/wtsq20

Bottom Line
   A journal that publishes research and case studies on the financial aspect of information. www.emeraldgrouppublishing.com/products/journals/journals.htm?id=bl

College and Research Libraries
   The journal of the Association of College and Research Libraries (ACRL). https://crl.acrl.org/index.php/crl

College and Research Libraries News
   The official news magazine of ACRL. https://crln.acrl.org/index.php/crlnews/index

Journal of Academic Librarianship
   A peer-reviewed journal that focuses on issues pertaining to college and university libraries. www.journals.elsevier.com/the-journal-of-academic-librarianship

Library Collections, Acquisitions, & Technical Services
    A journal that focuses on issues pertaining to collection management and technical services. *www.tandfonline.com/loi/ulca20*

Library Resources & Technical Services (LRTS)
    The official journal of the former ALA division the Association for Library Collections and Technical Services (ALCTS). *https://journals.ala.org/index.php/lrts*

Collection Management
    A quarterly journal that covers all aspects of collection development and management. *www.tandfonline.com/loi/wcol20*

The Serials Librarian
    A journal that covers topics related to the management of print and electronic serials. *www.tandfonline.com/loi/wser20*

PROFESSIONAL LISTSERVS

Collib-L
The official discussion list of the College Libraries Section (CLS) of the Association of College and Research Libraries (ACRL). *www.ala.org/acrl/aboutacrl/directoryofleadership/sections/cls/clswebsite/collibldisc/collibldiscussion*

ERIL-L
A discussion list for electronic resources. *www.eril-l.org/*

SERIALST
A moderated discussion forum about print and electronic serials. *www.nasig.org/*

TSLIBRARIANS
A listserv hosted by Kent State University for Technical Service Librarians and Catalogers. *TSLIBRARIANS@LISTSERV.KENT.EDU*

ULS-L
A listserv for the University Libraries section of ACRL. *http://lists.ala.org/sympa/info/uls-l*

PROFESSIONAL CONFERENCES AND ORGANIZATIONS

CORE: Leadership, Infrastructure, Futures
A new division of the American Library Association formed from former ALA divisions the Association for Library Collections & Technical Services (ALCTS), the Library and Information Technology Association (LITA), and the Library Leadership & Management Association (LLAMA). Core covers technical services, leadership, management, and technology in libraries. *https://core.ala.org/*

Charleston Conference
Held the first weekend of November in Charleston, SC, this conference is not attached to any professional organization. It is a conference for librarians, publishers and vendors to come together to discuss topics that focus on technical services and collection development. *https://charlestonlibraryconference.com*

Electronic Resources & Libraries (ER&L)
Held every year in Austin, Texas, this conference focuses on issues surrounding the management of electronic resources. *www.electroniclibrarian.org/conference-info/*

NASIG
Annual conference focusing on the management of electronic resources. Location of conference changes each year. *https://nasig.org/Conference*

Acquisitions Institute
Held every year outside of Portland, Oregon, this conference brings together librarians, publishers, and vendors to discuss topics related to acquisitions and collection development. *https://acquisitionsinstitute.org/*

CHAPTER **SIX**

Conclusion

Library acquisitions work involves many steps and processes from bibliographic searching, ordering, accounting, budgeting, invoicing, and payment, to name a few. The processes taken to procure materials for a library varies greatly from one library to the next, determined by the electronic systems used, institutional policies, and delineation of work within the unit. While there are many resources available to help you become knowledgeable about acquisitions, there is a fair amount of knowledge that will be learned on the job. Learning about institutional procedures and processes will account for a significant portion of the knowledge needed to manage acquisitions within a specific library.

Like other areas of librarianship, acquisitions is impacted by changes occurring within libraries today. This puts acquisitions in a unique position of being able to assist in the provision of new services. Acquisitions therefore requires flexibility, adaptability, and at times, out-of-the-box thinking as library processes change, technology changes, and formats acquired change. As Jesse Holden notes in *Acquisitions Core Concepts and Practices* (2018), acquisitions is taking on many activities outside of the core function of traditional acquisitions work. This is particularly evident as libraries move toward more purchase-on-demand models and incorporate public service areas like interlibrary loan into the acquisition process. Staffing in libraries is also undergoing transformations where new positions may emerge from a combination of positions due to retirements or because a new function requires new staff. As the nature of acquisitions evolves, it becomes imperative to develop strong habits of keeping abreast of changes along with continual inquiry. There are many resources available to help you acquire the knowledge needed to understand and successfully perform the work of acquisitions. This *Sudden Position Guide to Acquisitions* is intended to provide a place to start for those just learning about acquisitions, and to serve as a resource to keep current with the changing acquisitions landscape.

About the Authors

DEBORAH HATHAWAY is the Acquisitions and Collection Development Librarian for the University of Dallas. Deborah has fourteen years of experience working in acquisitions for the University of Dallas. She holds a BS in Human Relations and Business (Amberton University) and a Master's in Library Science (Texas Woman's University).

PAUL KELSEY is the Head of Acquisitions at Sims Memorial Library at Southeastern Louisiana University (2012-present). He previously served as the Agriculture Librarian and Social Sciences and Humanities Collection Development Coordinator for the LSU Libraries and Circulation Librarian for Penrose Library at Whitman College. He also has a number of years of experience working in public libraries. Paul recently served as co-chair of the former ALCTS Collection Management Section (CMS) Publications Committee and has past service on several other ALA and USAIN (United States Agricultural Information Network) committees. Paul holds a BA in Religion from The Colorado College, and his Master's in Library and Information Science from the University of Texas at Austin.

STACEY MARIEN has been the Acquisitions Librarian at American University in Washington, DC for over ten years. Prior to that position, she served as the Business Librarian at American for ten years and the Business Librarian at Elon University (formerly Elon College) for three years. Stacey holds a BA in Humanistic Studies (McGill University, Montreal, PQ, Canada), a Master's in Business Administration (University of Massachusetts, Boston), and a Master's of Science in Library Science (University of North Carolina, Chapel Hill).

SERIES EDITOR

SUSAN THOMAS served as the ALCTS Monographs Editor from 2015 to 2020. She is the Director of Collection Services for the Schurz Library and Subject Librarian for the Health Sciences at Indiana University South Bend. Susan has twenty-nine years of experience working in academic libraries. Prior to her current position at IU South Bend, Susan served as the Facilitator for Reference Services (1997–2004) and Archivist (1995–1997) at Valdosta State University (Georgia); the Assistant Head of the Regents Center Library and Bibliographer for Social Welfare at the University of Kansas/Edwards Campus; and as a Medical Reference Librarian at the University of Oklahoma Health Sciences Center Library. Susan holds a BA in Psychology (Indiana University), a Master's in Library and Information Science (Indiana University), and a Master's in Public Affairs (Indiana University South Bend).

CPSIA information can be obtained
at www.ICGtesting.com
Printed in the USA
JSHW041100201220
10398JS00002B/33